RAPID CHANGE
IMMEDIATE ACTION
FOR THE IMPATIENT LEADER

RAPID CHANGE
IMMEDIATE ACTION
FOR THE IMPATIENT LEADER

JOE LAIPPLE

Performance Management Publications (PMP)

Performance Management Publications (PMP)
3344 Peachtree Road NE, Suite 1050
Atlanta, GA 30326
678.904.6140
www.PManagementPubs.com

ISBN-13: 978-0-937100-23-3

ISBN-10: 0-937100-23-4

2 3 4 5 6 7

Cover and text Design: James Omedo
Production Coordinator: Laura-Lee Glass

PMP books are available at special discounts for bulk purchases
by corporations, institutions, and other organizations.
For more information, please call 678.904.6140, ext. 131 or e-mail
info@aubreydaniels.com

DEDICATION

To Hayne W. Reese
Scholar of successful working

RAPID CHANGE
IMMEDIATE ACTION
FOR THE IMPATIENT LEADER

PREFACE
AUTHOR'S NOTE

The point of this book is to help improve the influence of managers and leaders in implementing and achieving meaningful change—especially in helping others be more successful. The approach, derived from behavioral science, is from the perspective of the practitioner. The focus is on how to translate the science of behavior change so that it can be used quickly, easily and with impact. This book includes lessons for anyone who is looking to change their own behavior, influence the behavior of others or create long-term culture change. Those interested in the research that guides this work should refer to other sources. Try starting with a landmark book by Aubrey Daniels, *Performance Management*, which is a touchstone for many books with similar emphasis on behavior analysis in the workplace.

The intention here is to provide enough science at the right time to guide you along the path to change. It is not an easy path and it will present some challenges along the way. The process is designed to help you get started quickly now, to help make it work after you get started and then to sustain positive change.

Joe Laipple
April 2012

ABOUT THE AUTHOR

Joe Laipple, Ph.D., specializes in getting change to occur and making it stick. He is a behavioral scientist who has over 20 years of practical experience designing and implementing change in over 50 companies as a consultant, coach and mentor. He has published experimental studies on how our practical problem solving, logic, learning and memory change over time. Joe is a Senior Vice President of Strategic Services with Aubrey Daniels International specializing in implementation, leadership, coaching and culture change. He is the author of *Precision Selling*, a book on sales coaching.

SECTION I

CHANGE OVERVIEW

This section focuses on a simple connection—if you want to bring about sustainable long-term changes in *results,* start now with making incremental *behavior* changes that will lead to desired long-term outcomes. This section covers the experiences many have had when trying to bring about change not only within organizations but when trying to address personal change. It includes examples from real leaders and the business outcomes they achieved by changing their own behavior, influencing change in others and enhancing the cultures they led.

The principles of rapid change are reviewed in this section. The long-term results and how you integrate them into change plans are discussed. This section ends with a review of the essential need for *touch points*—the brief, high-impact interactions among managers and employees that are needed to prompt, reinforce and support incremental change on a daily basis.

CHAPTER 1

PERSISTENT AND DELIBERATE IMPATIENCE

"*Rapid change?* I don't know exactly what it is, but I need it."

When change is needed, we want it now. The idea of rapid change speaks to us at a gut level. It is appealing to any of us who have tried to bring about change in ourselves or others and have encountered the challenges to bringing about change and doing so quickly. It's when a leader confesses, "We have to find a way to do this faster or we won't survive." The idea of rapid change speaks to the part of us that is very impatient. Producing change immediately that is meaningful and sustainable requires more than wishful thinking. The process you will learn here is a science-based approach on how to produce the behaviors that are required to achieve desired outcomes. The behavioral focus gives you something to do actively with your impatience.

Most approaches to personal and organizational change are misguided in their design and execution. They leave out a most critical factor when they describe change—

how to manage human performance under such conditions. They assume that changes in vision and requests made of workers will somehow lead to the desired state. Existing habits are often ignored and the conditions under which work has been done are interrupted only by mandates and speeches about the need to change. Focusing on telling people what to do and hoping to inspire change without looking at the ways in which the daily behaviors are actually changing is not enough.

Big Bang . . . and Then a Whimper

Leaders spend a lot of time describing and imagining the future. The hoped for change is difficult, far off and overwhelming. If you only focus on the distant end-state, you usually do nothing today since you can always start tomorrow. At every Sunday dinner, my grandmother used to say as we were all eating her delicious spaghetti, meatballs, pork ribs and fresh baked bread that she was going to start a diet on Monday. She was always about to start her diet but she never took that first step. Many companies approach change like my grandmother.

You have seen some of the following scenarios up close and personal.

Leaders make great speeches in the beginning about the new vision and direction. Excitement and fanfare ensue. Resources are allocated to make the change happen. Expensive and time-consuming expert analyses are conducted. Painfully honest descriptions of the current state are reviewed. Promises and commitments are made. Then six months later, things are about the same and those great words ring hollow. What happened? When they got to the hard work of change, leaders and employees who started with good intentions lost their enthusiasm and returned to the habits that were working well enough, thank you very much. Eventually, someone decides that a different direction is better and the cycle starts over again with another round of great speeches with slightly different words and visions for a great future.

***

Employees go to training and hear about what they should do. The company invests and trains everyone on the new way of doing things. A small number of enthusiastic people take to the new training and find value in it. A few others deliberately continue to do things the old way. Many try the new skill and when it doesn't work right away or when it doesn't appear to work as well as what they already do, drop the new way and go back to their old habits. Some find a few things that work and use a few small changes to refine what they are already doing. Leaders discover people who are not doing what they were taught to do. These leaders may send people back to training or blame the training organization for not training people properly. Eventually, they will discover a new program and revisit this cycle again.

***

The company spends a lot of money on new technology. The new technology may be a computer system to integrate current tools. The initial system may be Version 1 and people are asked to use Version 2, even though they've become expert at Version 1. Now they have to make the switch, and they do so slowly and reluctantly. Someone may even say, "They are going to have to make me do it by taking away the old system. This new system doesn't work that well for me yet." An oft heard refrain from leadership goes something like this—"We spent $20 million on that new system. They better start using it!"

***

The company thought it had enhanced the quality of all work processes, yet business results have not changed that much. Programs that focus on processes and quality like lean manufacturing, Six Sigma, and others have a track record of putting process and structural changes in place (like standards for how work is done, how meetings are conducted and the steps one must take to do a job properly) that often become more about passing the test than improving the business. Employees may have complied with the standards, had an agenda and checked all the boxes in the checklist but none of these change business results. Changing a process doesn't guarantee changes in critical business behaviors.

Other examples follow a similar path—old way versus new way, current habits versus new behaviors, where you are now versus a promising future. Something is missing between point A and point B. You get to that desired future state quickly by creating a path of clear steps from A to B. It is necessary to understand what happens as people do things differently. That is where the truth of change resides—in whether or not persistent new patterns of behavior are built *and* sustained.

The most common path to change doesn't work well. The traditional path overemphasizes lengthy planning, great speeches, telling people what to do, securing compliance, focusing on results without looking at behavior, pointing fingers and failing to follow up and follow through. It includes good intentions but this is not enough. When you demand compliance, you'll get it only when you are looking. Real sustainable change will remain elusive.

The most effective path utilizes the principles of rapid change. Managers engage in brief planning about the change they want. Training and feedback are skill-based, in-the-moment with just the right amount of information to get started. Personal and persistent follow-up ensures development of habits to keep the changes going over time. The process emphasizes sharing good examples and specifically-defined events called *touch points*. This path includes a true understanding and application of positive reinforcement to help get change started, where individuals modify the changes over time and the targeted changes become habits. It promotes optimal performance rather than mere compliance. It develops individuals who are self-managed and who take full ownership of the change. It builds on what is working. It takes daily effort, but evidence of daily progress in the new behaviors will be seen along this path. It is guided by a repeatable technology derived from the science of human behavior and performance potential.

The path to rapid change also is populated by impatient individuals. Rapid change however requires one to demonstrate *deliberate impatience*. This is achieved through patience for attaining long-term results balanced with an obsessive impatience for the near-term behaviors needed to get change to occur now, tomorrow, next week and next month.

Turning this general impatience into a *persistent, deliberate* impatience requires:

1. Focusing very specifically on a few key behaviors to create meaningful change now, that add up to the long-term business results you really need in the end.
2. Identifying which behavior changes now will make the biggest difference over time.
3. Understanding and applying positive reinforcement effectively.

4. Using good examples that are hiding in plain sight.

5. Tweaking and fine-tuning along the way.

6. Holding back from ineffective demands—such as insisting that all behaviors change now—while developing the persistent patience required to achieve significant and sustained results.

Behavior Change Now

Rather than focus on desired results, attend to what people are saying and doing today that leads to desired long-term changes. If you understand behavior and its connection to results, you will be able to see when the right behaviors are creating the right results. You understand that it makes sense to be patient about the long term because you are seeing evidence of promising behavior changes today that are moving in the right direction. It will also help you know when to exert your impatience and say "This is not working" so that you can make deliberate adjustments as needed.

Positive Reinforcement is Not What You Think It Is

One of the keys to ensuring that change not only occurs but that it sticks *is positive reinforcement.* Positive reinforcement is misunderstood in significant ways. Many leaders, when asked to describe positive reinforcement, typically mention money or pats on the back. While these are potential examples of positive reinforcement, they are not the ones most likely to get change to continue and stick over time. The types of positive reinforcement that will help the most are more immediate and certain and are what behavior analysts call *natural consequences*. Understanding this is essential if rapid change is desired. Some key words that provide clues to change happening or being blocked are worth considering here. If we have two options and one is fun, easy, simple, fast and requires less effort, that option will be more likely to occur and stick. The option that is boring, tedious, slow, hard, complex and requires more effort is less likely to occur over time.

Clues for Consequences that Matter	
Increase Likelihood	**Decrease Likelihood**
Fun	Boring or Tedious
Easy	Hard
Simple	Complex
Less Work	More Work
Effortless	Effortful
Quick	Slow

A simple example illustrates what this means. The iPhone, introduced in 2007, was engineered in a way that has many of the consequences lined up in its favor. Using it, even the first time, is easy, fun, cool, simple, and quick—some might even say intuitive. Apple's engineers have been running this same play with their technology for years.

This is a challenge. Most approaches to change don't

have the kind of engineering that is built into the iPhone. Instead, we are faced with a period of time when we have to stick with something until it gets fun, easy, simple, and requires less time, work and effort. Managing this time period is essential for rapid change, and behavioral science has answers to help guide you through it. The challenge of course is that new and desired behaviors tend to require more time, work and effort in the beginning. Our old habits, on the other hand, tend to be effortless, and require less time and work. Putting the right kinds of positive reinforcement in place for the right kinds of behaviors is necessary to accelerate the rate of change over time.

Improving Your Organization is Hiding in Plain Sight

In most organizations people are so busy that they spend most of their time managing exceptions, addressing what is not working, putting out fires and doing post-mortems on projects. Leaders and employees spend the day looking for and talking about deviations. Individuals in these companies hide bad news until it is too late. Leaders have conversations with employees when something goes wrong.

Too much talk about what is *not* working merely tells us what not to do. Finding out what to do instead is necessary to achieve optimal performance. Traditionally, those who get good results are ignored during most of the year. Little effort is spent determining how these individuals got the results. Talking about how someone or some group improved their business results helps identify what others need to do to improve. Creating organizational competence in observing, describing and talking about behavior—the *how*—has economic merit and will help move you along the path to rapid change.

The 3-Minute Meeting™

Managing performers the traditional way includes long, formal conversations between boss and direct report. Traditional performance reviews and evaluations are dreaded by all involved. This approach is fundamentally flawed and can be replaced with *The 3-Minute Meeting*™, short conversations with employees on a frequent and ongoing basis. A specific technique used in rapid change is something called *touch points*—the brief coaching interactions that are intended to help employees improve.

How to Get the Change You Want

There is a science of change, primarily behavior analysis, translated for the practitioner and introduced in small segments throughout this book. Examples are used to show how that science has been applied by others and how it specifically works not in abstract terms but in concrete ways. Many of these situations will sound familiar and the examples provide specific ways to achieve sustainable change.

The first and most important issue relating to change is what you will do now. What are the small steps I can take today that will help now and move me one step closer to my desired end-state?

Once change is started, you will want to know how to keep going tomorrow. Part of the solution is to pick one to two things to do today that will allow you to see early signs of progress. Define *change* as what is needed to do today that you can see working *today*. Pick a few behaviors that you can see working . . . even just a little bit . . . today. Then fine-tune what you are doing so that the new things you try work better and better each day. The behavioral scientists call this *shaping* and without a solid understanding of it you are sunk. Those who end up achieving transformational change were really good at shaping. If you want transformational change, try getting good at shaping first.

Rapid change doesn't include getting advice from experts who tell you something you already know. Most people know that to lose weight, they need to exercise more and eat better. Content experts don't help when they overwhelm you with everything they know or with regurgitating what you already know.

The question is *how* do you move from knowing and understanding something to taking some action that leads to desired results and outcomes? This requires facilitating change rather than only being the mouthpiece for change. An effective behavioral approach helps identify what to start doing today that works, shows when to follow up and indicates which small changes are needed so that it works even better.

Eventually, you figure out how to do this on your own. If you only ask yourself the right questions, you can keep change going in the right direction and discover what works well. You can then discover other tweaks to improve what you are currently doing. This process—and it is a replicable process—of uncovering your own practical expertise and shaping your own change on a daily basis is one of the keys to achieving *rapid change.*

Describing Rapid and Change

Rapid means *now.* Though long-term results are not immediately attainable, you can have *behavior* changes today. Changes in leader behaviors should be designed to cause and influence changes in employee behaviors . . . not later, but today. The new employee behaviors are intended to bring about incremental changes in internal and external customer behaviors today. The challenge is identifying and defining what these behavior changes are, how you sequence them and how you build these changes over time to add up to the results you want. So what can change rapidly?—*what you do and say today.*

Improving business results requires changes in behavior. The change that most leaders want is in business results. The bottom line really is the bottom line. Changes business leaders want usually include improvement in some financial result. It is business after all. The long-term results companies worry about are the ones rapid change is designed to address.

The next chapter includes a workplace example that challenged the traditional approach to change and led to the development of rapid change methods. It includes the principles that are embodied in this book and will revolutionize your workplace. What follows will take you steps closer to mastering the art and science of achieving rapid behavior change to make a real difference in the commitment, excitement and impact of your workplace.

CHAPTER 2

PRINCIPLES THAT WORK

Good examples and stories are essential to creating and sustaining change. Examples will be used in each chapter to illustrate specifically how incremental behavior change leads to results changes. They serve to show how to do this well, how to replicate it with your own challenges and desired changes, and how to accelerate the rate of change. They will help you skip steps so that you can change faster and learn what has worked for someone else that presumably will work for you. These good examples provide a path forward that can help speed up the changes needed to achieve success. Let's start with the real-life example that prompted the writing of this book.

A Model of Deliberate Impatience —Mike's Story

This example includes several elements that help to start a change and get it to stick. It includes a way to accelerate the pace of change, get something started now that works and leads to the long-term outcomes you want, and provides a way to do so effectively and efficiently.

Mike is a take-charge leader in a large, financial services organization. Initially he was the head of sales for this organization. The company I work for brought some of the basics of the science of behavior change to the workplace such as providing feedback and reinforcement for valued behaviors. Mike had seen the science work in his organization but he wanted to find a way to make it work faster, because the business environment wasn't good and it was getting worse and he needed to get better results quickly.

He had several thousand employees to influence, so he challenged his team to find ways to get change to occur faster across a wider range of people. Mike had a remarkable ability to be focused with very deliberate impatience on the kinds of business outcomes he was attacking and the kinds of behaviors at all levels that he needed in order to make real and sustainable changes. Many of the things he did were elements that are essential if you want to achieve rapid change. Mike implemented change in his organization by bringing about action rather than wasting time with lip service just talking about change.

Leader as Careful Observer

Mike and his direct reports used to make comments about the note-taking I did at their monthly senior meetings. I write down what I hear people saying and what I see people doing. These observations include who asks what questions and the kinds of answers these questions receive. My role was to provide feedback at the end of the meeting to help the team of leaders improve how they approached their follow-up. Before the leaders returned to their regional offices, I described to the group what I liked about the meeting and offered a few suggestions that I hoped were helpful. The recommendations were based on observations within the meeting or within the actual workplace.

The feedback included primarily what I liked and also included things that didn't work, always including a suggestion about how to improve. Several leaders stated specifically how helpful the feedback was. Initially, I felt good about the value I was providing in the sessions. I felt that I was earning the right to be there time and time again. After a few meetings like this, Mike started to observe more carefully and specifically during these meetings and when he visited different work sites.

Mike became very good at observing and taking objective notes on what he saw and heard. He wrote down specific behaviors or *pinpoints* and developed a strong ability to capture key information. Around this time, Mike began offering his feedback at the meetings before I did, sharing it in the same format described earlier. He would carefully observe what was said or done and then he'd write it down, later sorting through his observations and highlighting what he liked. He then formulated the top two to three things he'd like to see modified or changed. Mike started to give extremely clear and helpful feedback. I no longer had to do any of that. Mike was demonstrating the key behaviors and principles of what would become rapid change by doing something useful with his observations.

During one meeting Mike covered most of the key points that I was going to cover, so I almost gulped when he asked me to share my observations and offer a few additional recommendations. I initially said that Mike took all of my key points but then I took a step back, shared a few observations, and then offered a few refinements and additions. I learned several things that day. One was that Mike was a very good observer. He almost always focused on the right things, and he described his observations clearly and objectively to his team.

I shared this insight with Mike and his team at the next meeting. I pointed out that Mike offered very good feedback the last time and he based much of that on his observations and subsequent notes. Mike encouraged his team of leaders to capture their observations more carefully this time. He asked them to be a bit more active as they listened to the issues covered, writing down what they liked along with any suggestions to improve the business or the performance of the team.

Careful and objective observations of behavior are part of the foundation of effective feedback loops and rapid change. Leaders who are careful, objective observers and who take notes, put themselves in a position to offer clear and helpful feedback regarding what they want and what they don't want. Doing so also helps them identify what is actually happening in their workplace.

Discover Exactly What You Want

Mike knew what he wanted in the near term and the long term. However, when he was put in charge of a collections organization, he really started to get impatient with the speed of change. He wanted improvement in losses and in the 30-, 60-, and 90-day delinquency numbers. He also knew that he couldn't just play the numbers game with these results. He wanted more than just improvement in the numbers. He wanted the quality of the collections calls to improve. He used to say, "The calls don't lie." The team would listen to the calls and ask "Is this a quality call? Is this the kind of product—the call—that we as a leadership team want to stand behind? Are the behaviors the most effective in collecting money sooner rather than later?" The answer to every one of those questions was a resounding *no.*

Initially, no one could find an example of what a good call sounded like, and they listened to a lot of calls. The more calls they listened to, the worse they felt. So Mike asked his group of leaders in the field to listen to calls as well. The goal was to find one or two calls that could be used as examples to create the specific desired changes. After all, they couldn't just continue to listen to a bunch of bad calls and expect any change.

They finally found two samples of good calls. Mike made the final decisions not just on what his long-term vision was but on what *good* sounded and looked like *today*. The two calls brought an extreme focus to what was desired across the organization. The calls were used to further pinpoint behaviors and break down what a good call sounded like. The calls were taped and shared across the organization. Individuals would listen to the calls in groups and would discuss what they were hearing. Leadership used the recorded calls as examples of desired behavior for others who were on the phones, for supervisors who managed the people on the phones, for the quality team who listened and evaluated calls and for trainers who trained new and existing employees on what good calls sounded like.

The two good calls were used to create a short list of the four key behaviors for improving a call. If individuals were getting by on their old, bad habits, we weren't going to break those habits by giving them 25 things to do. We needed to break the call down into its component parts, starting with four key behaviors. We also helped the employees sequence the four behaviors so that they became good at each behavior in the order of when they should occur on the call. For example, the first behavior in the sequence was to state the total amount due and ask for it *today*. When this was used to start a call, it helped get to the point of the call more quickly and with greater clarity. The goal was to help people get good at the basics before mastering more complicated things like negotiating.

Persistent and Deliberate Impatience

How do you ensure you not only get change to occur but get it to stick? One way is to be persistent in your follow-up and deliberate with your impatience for doing the behaviors now that demonstrate real change. Mike is a master at deliberate impatience. He is a numbers guy but he realizes that in order to get consistently better numbers, he needs to focus on improvement in the right behaviors.

Part of this deliberate impatience is giving people permission to stop doing the things now that are getting in the way of being effective. Don't just add new priorities on top of all the other priorities that people have. How do you help others sort through the new and the current priorities to make good decisions about a workable and balanced daily plan? Mike was able to help people shift their priorities—*this now, not that.* He was able to see behaviors that were getting in the way and was able to tell people in objective terms what they were doing that was an old, bad habit. Importantly, he was also able to articulate what they needed to do instead. The clarity of Mike's observational skills made it almost impossible for his people to mislead him, and it also made him an ideal person for focusing on what mattered and for bringing about real, sustainable change.

Mike's story and the stories of other leaders in this book serve as concrete examples to help solve problems and get desired changes to occur now. These stories include principles of change that will be explored next. They also provide guideposts for any leader who is attempting to not just get change to occur quickly but to get it to stick.

Principles of Rapid Change

Rapid change requires a process that ensures that change not only occurs but sticks. Since the principles involved in the process of rapid change are derived from the science of human behavior they are adaptable to any change effort. These principles are at work in all behavior whether you acknowledge them or not. Since principles are applicable to many situations every attempt will be made throughout this book to relate them to practical work behavior. Examples like Mike's are included to illustrate how these principles are applied to real work problems.

When Mike asked to find a way to make things work faster, he was caught in what seemed like a no-win situation. The key word in his request for me was faster, because I realized that to him *faster* also meant better and to be better required more people involvement. He found success in influencing change with thousands of employees. He had clear successes he could point to and a body of evidence to show people where and how change had occurred. The principles listed below served to guide Mike and others who were attempting not just fast change, but the kind of change that involved more people and that had a measurable impact on business results that mattered.

Nine Principles of Rapid Change

1.	Start with a persistent, deliberate impatience.
2.	Maintain a clear line of sight.
3.	Observe and gather a body of evidence.
4.	Break performance into component behaviors.
5.	Do something different now.
6.	See it work.
7.	Fine-tune what you are doing.
8.	Practice with repetition.
9.	Develop positive accountability.

Let's shine additional light on the principles using practical terms for those trying to plan and follow up on personal or organizational changes. These principles can then be applied to new situations that you face. Change efforts that work and that are sustained include all of these principles and they usually occur during an implementation in the order listed here.

1. **Start with a persistent, deliberate impatience.** When needing to bring about change, pressure and impatience to get results accelerates over time. You may want the results now but you are unlikely to get them now. Impatience for the rate of change, especially in the beginning of any change effort, should be very calculated and controlled. A deliberate impatience can be leveraged to focus on getting started now and trying new and different things now. Start by identifying the behaviors and activities that will eventually lead to desired outcomes. Patience, unfortunately, is required for the ultimate outcomes. We all know this but that doesn't stop us from desiring immediate gratification. Shift attention, effort and impatience then to what is controllable. This deliberate impatience focused on behaviors may also fade when you don't see quick outcomes. In this situation it is easy to drop the ball and focus elsewhere. Persistence then is essential to ensure that not only do changes occur but that they also stick.

2. **Maintain a clear line of sight.** It helps to have a clear picture of desired outcomes and to know where you are going. This keeps the focus on the business value of the change. This line of sight also helps to keep day-to-day activities

focused on this as well. What will these changes today accomplish and add up to? Why am I doing this anyway? When will the team likely get there? What is the business case and long-term goal? Consider options for the defined goal and possible tactics that provide guidance along the way. Behavior is still the daily focus but the line of sight allows you to chart your direction. Develop a longer-term view to help guide what you are doing now. The long term is what you are being patient about today. This also helps to ensure that you don't become too focused on behaviors only. It's like when a checklist is developed to guide a change and the change drifts off course to completing the paperwork, rather than engaging in specific behaviors that achieve some business outcome. Activities and behaviors should help accomplish some business outcome. Articulate this outcome. Write it down. Draw a picture. It can help to provide a reminder of what all the extra effort is for. Some leaders will use the line of sight to continue to focus others on the behaviors that have not yet led to long-term business outcomes—the attempts at the new behaviors haven't yet achieved the long-term goals but you are getting better at them and in time they will help deliver on your long-term objectives. In this scenario, reinforce the attempts while keeping an eye on where this new behavior is likely to take you.

3. Observe and gather a body of evidence. Looking only at the long-term outcomes likely leads to constantly feeling discouraged. As each day goes by, the evidence may indicate that yet again you have not reached the long-term goals. This is why it is important to identify near-term indicators that are on the path to long-term goals. A near-term indicator might be the incremental progress in eating habits today when trying to lose weight. These *leading indicators* help determine if you are making progress. In some change efforts this could be what customers or others are experiencing as a result of the new behaviors that are being attempted. What happens today when you try the new behavior? What is different today? The immediate change might be someone trying something new and feeling comfortable trying it again. The leading indicators include behaviors that can be observed and measured today. Other leading indicators include activities and near-term results measures. Lagging results happen later presumably as a result of the leading indicators. A robust body of evidence includes tracking leading indicators and monitoring lagging results.

4. Break performance into component behaviors. One principle that will help achieve
rapid change is to break down a desirable performance into its component behaviors. This
includes describing the new behavior with
enough specificity and detail to ensure it happens and is correlated with the desirable near-
term and long-term impact. It also includes
refining the behavior to ensure it is clear, objective, and repeatable. This specificity is called
pinpointing. Identify a *pinpoint* you can focus
on that is likely to make a big difference in the
outcome. What small adjustment will you
make in your behavior today or this week that
is likely to bring about the biggest return on
the investment in time? Identify the small
change that you can make that will help the
most. Track it so you can then see it working.
This will likely encourage you to keep at it until
you get really good at this new change. When
you become fluent—get to habit strength—in
the new behavior, you can select another one
to change or improve.

5. Do something different now. "Do or do
not. There is no try." Yoda, the famous *Star
Wars* character, makes an important point. Yes,
the goal is to do it. The ease of doing nothing
presents the biggest challenge. When you hear
about change and it sounds promising, start

doing something now. Pick anything and see how it feels and how it works. Spending all of your time planning something big and then giving up when it gets too big is not the goal anyone has in mind. Coming up with a pretty plan or a complex one shouldn't be the goal either. Achieving changes in behaviors and outcomes are your targets. Delaying starting something until you get complete agreement is unlikely to get you where you want to be. Consider the task at hand. Do something with it today. Write something down. Take a first step. Get it started. Then you can reflect on how it felt and worked. Then take another step tomorrow to see how that feels and works. Don't wait for the exact right moment. There isn't likely to be one. The way most change efforts are planned and structured requires more persistent and consistent focus than is usually provided.

Delay in starting to change may be because you have too much on your plate. Or it may be because it interferes with an established routine. It may also be due to daily fires and crises that provide distraction. Look carefully at fires and crises. They may be putting up a smoke screen that masks the real issues and perpetuates the problems. Attention may be needed to redirect the efforts in clear and persistent ways. If you are only doing something monthly, you are unlikely to have success in reaching and sustaining the desired changes. Weekly, daily or hourly application and practice is required to connect what you are doing to the results you want.

"Do it" is the intent but is not the most effective way to get behavior change of others to occur when you aren't looking. It may work better when you use it on yourself as part of your internal dialogue. When you use a phrase like "do it" when managing others, you are acting like the boss. Telling someone to do it doesn't always translate into immediate action today. Some of us may be prompted to action when someone says "do it." Others may be more encouraged if you say, "You may not want to do this, but try it now and let's talk about how it worked." It will be impossible to reinforce a behavior that is not occurring. Set things up so that "trying" will be reinforced. It's like the old *Life* cereal commercial with Mikey—"Try it, you'll like it." In the early stages of change it is essential that you simply do something right now. You can worry about it working and having the desired impact after you have tried it a few times. Just give it a shot. Others don't even have to buy in, like it or agree it is a good thing to do.

6. See it work. Once something new is tried people can see whether or not it works. I'm not talking about achieving world peace here. I'm talking about small changes that lead to movement in the right direction, like taking the first step down the path. The "seeing it work" might be something like "That wasn't as bad as I thought it was going to be." A small change can be defined as something that seems easier, is less work or less effort, than anticipated. It might be that someone feels increasingly comfortable. It could be peers and customers saying that the effort is moving in the right direction. Teams could spend time debating the merits of something for days, weeks and months before they actually do it. Save some time and skip that debate. Encourage people to try it and then help them see it work as soon as possible. This isn't about a measurable result but about the kind of desirable reaction that is likely if the behavior takes place today.

7. Fine-tune what you are doing. Just trying it is a good place to start, but trying to make it *work* is even better for continuing it over time. The issue is "How are you regularly fine-tuning and tweaking something to make it work better?" Evidence that people are fine-tuning a behavior can tell you if change is occurring and moving beyond mere compliance. Encourage

others to fine-tune the change. Encourage others to make it work better.

8. **Practice with repetition.** Starting something new will likely be a challenge. Find a variety of ways to practice new behaviors. I'm not talking about perfect practice here. It would be great if everyone could be perfect the first time, but that is unlikely. Attempt to get it almost right before you attempt to go faster with it. Focus on quality practice before you speed it up. Focus on effective practice and then you can worry about being efficient. It not only takes practice but takes time and repetition to get good at anything new. If you were trying to develop fluency in driving a car, shooting free throws or mastering chess, it would be tough for you to develop those skills without frequent repetition. Repetition. Repetition. Repetition. Did I mention repetition?

9. **Develop Positive Accountability.** Sustainable change requires someone holding you accountable, even if it's just yourself. There needs to be some point at which there will be "an accounting." Who will you tell or show what you did relative to what you committed to do? In positive accountability the focus is necessarily on what has been accomplished rather than what was not done or what was not done well.

You may commit to try it, to see it work, to fine-tune it. What is committed to is unique to each person. Accountabilities are different for employees, managers and leaders. As employees the accountability may be to find ways to make the new approach work in a way that is productive, safe and high quality. Positive accountability won't work unless there are multiple opportunities where managers and leaders follow up, support and look at what is working. The focus here though is on what is working and for the attempts that lead to desirable outcomes. An important point more fully outlined later is that leaders have the opportunity to demonstrate positive accountability in brief, frequent coaching interactions—*touch points*—that guide and sustain change over time.

Avoid repeating the cycle of well-intended starts and then shifting direction when it doesn't seem like it is working. These principles, when applied to a change effort, can help break this cycle. It is not just change for the sake of change that is the goal. As it is in the case of business and investigative journalism, it usually comes down to following the money.

CHAPTER 3

THE BIG PILE OF MONEY

The challenge for leaders is that the answer to "What do you want?" is often described as a generic future state. Organizations aspire to similar long-term outcomes that involve various kinds of improvement. They may have a slightly new-and-improved definition of these outcomes such as *Trusted Advisor*, *Six Sigma*, or *Profit-Driven Company*. Organizations often pay big dollars for some group to help them figure out what they want to become. The answers are often generic, like motherhood and apple pie—hard to argue with, hard to disprove.

Granted, having a clear, long-term objective helps to keep change efforts rooted in a business outcome. Too many change efforts morph into becoming not about improving the business environment or reaching a business goal but about implementing the process and the details of the change effort.

Here's the deal. Most companies want to make more money or get more customers. Even when the talk is focused on something like *Trusted Advisor*, if you scratch the surface, the real issue is this—how can the company get more of that big pile of money? Let's not hide behind words. Companies are about making money. If this is the case, say so. Be clear on what the big pile of money means to you. It is like the pot of gold at the end of the rainbow. It is the end point that provides clarity and direction to keep us going each day, whether that end point is money, customer satisfaction, quality, safety, marketplace dominance or a balance of your important results.

It is helpful to have a clear business reason for any change initiative and to be honest about the reason while maintaining a clear line of sight, one of the principles described in Chapter 2. The problem with the big pile of money is that it isn't achieved right now. It doesn't just magically happen. It doesn't appear just because someone wants it. Without a clear business purpose, the current work will be easy to scrap and someone will come up with the next big change initiative. Keep in mind that with the right behavior changes now, the big pile of money will be produced and earned later.

Besides spending a lot of time and effort describing the future state, companies almost inevitably take another step. They identify what frontline employees need to do to make it all happen. This may involve any or all of the following—a new and improved process, enhanced training, a new procedure, additional job aids and tools. The company then falsely frames the problem and solution as two primary factors—a clearly described end-state and a focus on employee behaviors that presumably will help achieve this outcome. Framing a problem this way is a mistake. It makes the leader role as primarily on the front end defining the vision, mission and strategy. It makes the frontline employee role one of doing something different over a period of time that is needed to bring about this long-term outcome. When it doesn't work six months later, fingers are pointed at a few leaders who selected the wrong strategy. Or employees are blamed for not implementing the plan or not buying into the process or not doing what they needed to do to bring about the desired changes. When designing change in a way that omits accountability and follow-up from leadership and management on an ongoing and active basis, leaders are leaving out of the change process the elements that will help ensure that the change doesn't just occur once, but that it will also stick.

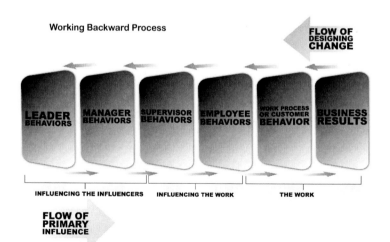

The Working Backward graphic on the previous page shows a fuller picture of the desired results changes and the connections to behaviors that lead to the results. It is called *working backward* because the starting point is some desired result and the change is designed by identifying what is needed from each key player after first identifying the long-term result. The behaviors taken together and in sequence from customer to employee to management are required to achieve these results. It is designed from right to left. It is **reverse behavioral engineering** in the design phase.

- What customer behaviors will create the desired results? It might be a "Yes" response or "I need to know more" from the customer.

- What employee behaviors are likely to create these customer outcomes? Possible behaviors include asking questions, listening to internal or external customer needs or sharing information.

- What then do employees need from their supervisors to help them demonstrate the necessary behaviors? It is likely some kind of helpful coaching.

During implementation, the behaviors typically provide influence from left to right. Framing the problem and solution as an end-state that depends only on employee behaviors focuses only on results and what employees need to do to accomplish this change.

Follow-up is needed to keep the changes going and to ensure that they stick. The employee behaviors that are happening today don't immediately lead to the results later. They are influenced by customers, sometimes on an hourly basis. The influence is strongest, most immediate and most frequent from internal and external customers rather than management. Leaders, managers and supervisors are essential then to guiding change over a sustained period of time. In order to ensure change, the connections among these boxes cannot be left to chance. Leaders, managers and supervisors have an ongoing role to get change started and to follow up, help and encourage it along the way.

To achieve a successful outcome, it is necessary to define the problem of change beyond just results and employee behaviors. Part of the solution to this challenge is planning a better path to get there and better connections between behaviors and results. Let's look at a few brief examples that illustrate this dilemma.

The New Sales Process

Many organizations ask for help in implementing a new sales process. Here's what usually happens.

From the leadership perspective, the old sales process isn't working as they had hoped. Salespeople aren't closing. Salespeople aren't planning. Salespeople skip steps in the current process. The pre-work is lacking.

The follow-up work is nonexistent. Positive customer feedback may have taken a dip.

Then someone reads a book or goes to a workshop or hears about the latest fad. That someone concludes that the problem is with the current sales process. They then decide to invest time, effort and money in a new one. "Changing the current sales process will automatically solve our problem—employees will plan, employees will do difficult things, employees will close, employees will follow up and employees will do administrative work after the job is done."

Next, someone takes a big leap and persuades leaders to invest in a new sales process. A few months later they discover that they still have some of the same problems. People aren't following the new process either. Employees still aren't planning and doing pre-call work. They aren't doing the tough work during the call. They aren't closing. They aren't doing the follow-up as expected. They aren't doing the required post-call work.

Leaders are getting impatient over the lack of use of the new process. Others may send mixed signals and ask salespeople to do whatever it takes to get the numbers up this month, even if it means skipping parts of the sales process. Leaders send other kinds of mixed signals. They may push their employees to deliver reports on the activity captured in the new sales process and the sales results. In these cases, they learn later that people found a few shortcuts around both the new sales process and sales reporting. No one will catch on any time soon.

What someone thought was a good idea just created more problems. What was missing from their plan?

The New Computer System

The current technology works, but it doesn't work that well. It is too slow or requires a work-around or it is simply not cutting edge. "The biggest difference between us and our competitors," someone concludes, "is that they have better technology. If we only replaced our old technology, we'd catch up. Besides, we aren't using the current technology like we should anyway."

So they spend big bucks on a new system. The new system is sleeker and better than the current system. The old system may have duct tape on it. It may be antiquated. It certainly could work better but employees have discovered work-arounds to the problems, even if they have to use five or more programs just to do the job. Imagine having five programs open at once when dealing with customers. Employees use Post-it notes to jot things down.

Yet work is getting done in this current state. Employees have figured out adaptive ways to be successful. The new system will cost big bucks but the old system works fine enough. The investment is finally made. However, the company may not be able to shut down the old system yet. Despite all the bells and whistles of the new system, employees still choose to use the old system. The new system eventually will work better but employees avoid using it. They even complain about parts of it. Managers may be blindly telling their employees to use only the new system. Customers suffer and then employees say that managers care more about the new system than the customers.

What typically happens is this—There is great fanfare when the new system is launched. Hours are spent in training employees how to use it. The manual looked good. When the trainer showed how to use the new system, it looked easy enough. When employees use the new system, they may be slower right now in using it so when management gets impatient, they may start to put the pressure on employees for getting the job done fast. Later employees go back to the old system. They know they can get the job done fast and right that way. What did they miss as they navigated the change?

Improving Safety in the Workplace

Our safety numbers can be better. The lagging safety results, like incidents and injuries, need improvement. Senior leadership makes statements about wanting a safer workplace. Someone concludes that a change in the frontline employees' behavior would help bring about the change. The change often comes in the form of a program that addresses safety primarily for frontline employees. There may be training and a program put in place. It involves a checklist or some form of observing for frontline employees. Meetings are scheduled and committees are established. Teams are put in place to increase employee involvement. There may be an initial focus and observed improvement. The lagging results look good for now. People make improvements not only to the work but to how safely they do the work. There is initial progress.

A few months later productivity drops and then it is all hands on deck. Employees at every level return to the old shortcuts that helped them in the past. Managers are now placing more emphasis on productivity. Those shortcuts work well enough, no one has been hurt yet, and the focus can now be on how to improve productivity. Employees who take those shortcuts and who are showing improvements in productivity are encouraged and reinforced. Once again our safe practices are slipping. This kind of pattern is bound to lead to some accidents and incidents in the future. Then it will be back to the drawing board to re-address safety after that happens.

What was forgotten as they tried to implement this change?

The previous examples illustrate some of the many different faces of change initiatives and why they don't work—employees won't try a new way of doing things or they take shortcuts, management doesn't positively reinforce or follow up on change efforts and often, the wrong system or behavior is targeted for change.

Returning to the Big Pile of Money

Let's return now to the big pile of money. A specific end-point is the goal. Find out where the big pile of money is in any sustainable change initiative—is it more money, more productivity, a safer workplace, better quality work? It usually is a balance of result outcomes—more revenue *and* satisfied customers, productive *and* safe, productive *and* high quality. It is not just making money no matter what the damage to others. Where do you eventually want to be? What is the future state many months from now? What do you want the change effort, change initiative, sales process, computer system or safety program to accomplish months down the road? After clearly defining the primary purpose, then anchor the activities and behaviors today to what you really want to accomplish. Once this is done, begin to identify what can be done today and what outcomes those actions and behaviors are likely to accomplish today—outcomes that will eventually add up to that big pile of money. The behaviors here require involvement not just from frontline employees, but also include supervisors, managers, leaders and customers. Knowing the desired, balanced, long-term outcome is one step. How you get there is also as important. It is not about getting results any way you can. It requires selecting and implementing the right, desirable behaviors that create the right, long-term outcomes.

This process provides a path of incremental steps along the way that lead to the big pile of money. Shape behaviors today so that these behaviors achieve what is intended. Each of us has a specific accountability for the elements of change that are within our control rather than all of us being accountable for everything. Certainly an end-point is needed, but a clear path and some good steps along the way where success can be defined daily or weekly will help. Identify now the desirable impact on others today, this week and this month that indicates if there is movement toward that big pile of money.

CHAPTER 4

TOUCH POINTS— RAPID COACHING

Thomas Gilbert in his book *Human Competence* wrote, "There are great differences in what people accomplish, but small differences in their repertoires of behavior." I believe that Gilbert was describing the difference that persistent, small, but significant differences in refining our behaviors make in determining whether or not you achieve your long-term goals.

Good leaders demonstrate a persistence of effort and a constant scrutiny of improvement in the small steps that make change possible. It is how effective leaders express the principle of positive accountability for change. For some, this type of leadership does appear to come naturally but it is a skill that can be learned. Let me describe the example of John, a person whom I view as an exemplary leader. He was a master at the brief, helpful coaching interactions—the touch points—that are essential for influencing others and creating a culture that helps employees and ensures optimal performance.

Touch Points that Help—John's Story

John is the best example of a leader who knows how to build followership and who is able to use brief, frequent, genuine touch points among his team of direct reports. He is also a leader who is extremely clear on his long-term vision—his line of sight. Let's start with what his followers did that was notable. The people on John's team consistently operated at a high-and-steady rate of performance. Individuals consistently gave discretionary effort—went beyond the call of duty—even in times of difficulty and stress (more details about discretionary effort will be provided in Chapter 5). Employees trusted John and his managers. They were also willing to tell the truth to John and to other leaders.

If you followed John around at a national meeting you would see him pull people aside, look them in the eye and talk to them about what was happening in their world. He not only asked about the work they were doing but also about the events of their personal lives.

At one time John reviewed a survey that looked at some of his leadership behaviors. The survey was done online and produced several reports and graphs. People provided feedback to John based on 15 or so statements on his effectiveness. This included things like the clarity of his expectations, how often he provided feedback and coaching, how he helped and how he communicated. Direct reports also had an opportunity to describe what they'd like him to start, stop and continue doing. I didn't realize how seriously he took the feedback until he showed up to the meeting when both of us were reviewing the feedback with his team. They were getting feedback from their team of direct reports too. He brought previous feedback he had gotten across his career going back over 10 years and made copies for the group. He showed them verbatim what people said about him, how he made progress and some areas where he still needed improvement. He was a little disappointed that his team didn't give him more details on what he could do differently to enhance his leadership. He pushed his team to give him a bit more detail and to offer more suggestions on how he could improve. He helped them describe that in a very careful and safe way by asking questions that went beyond general feedback and he probed his team with follow-up questions to pinpoint specific behaviors that he should continue to do or specific behaviors that he should modify to improve his impact.

The feedback they initially gave him on the survey was a little bit biased because they liked him so much. He didn't want that to get in the way of becoming an even better leader. This modeling of asking for more feedback and helping his team share more specific feedback, especially what he could change or improve, was eye-opening for all of us. After I saw what he did, I thought, "So that's how you do that." John's actions defined leadership transparency. "Here's what people have said about me over the years. I'm a big boy, and I can take it. I think I *can* handle the truth . . . and so can you." It also demonstrated what truth-telling can look like in a company. If you want your team to be truthful just how might you model that? John was able to create that foundation of trust that is a prerequisite for attaining meaningful change.

Let's look at what John does—his leader behavior—to help him create this kind of impact.

1. John is masterful at the art of brief, three-minute interactions with his people (*The 3-Minute Meeting*™). His primary skill is in asking great questions to get people talking. This isn't so much about coaching to change behavior as it is about asking questions to convey genuine interest in others. When he's with employees at national meetings, when he visits them in the field, or when he speaks to them on the phone he takes the time to have them describe the good things that they accomplished. He conveys interest and helps his people share the details of what they did to accomplish each outcome.

2. He has extremely high standards for himself and his team. These high expectations are not just for the results but for how people get results.

The *how* matters. In John's case the *how* required adhering to the strong work ethic that people had on his team.

3. John comes armed with a good memory for what people have said in the past and other details about their lives.

4. He consistently asks for feedback both before and after key moments. He uses the feedback to make the small changes that are likely to make the biggest impact.

5. He does his homework and over-prepares. Most people don't know how much time he puts into presentations, selecting just the right words. John once told me that others may be smarter than him but they'd never out-prepare him.

6. John finds ways to build fun into the work. That fun could be enjoying a good meal or a good glass of wine together after work. The fun could also be events like listening to music together or riding mechanical bulls or going bowling. He isn't afraid of making fun of himself and stresses the togetherness of the group. You don't have to do everything, but you do have to show up and be part of it.

There is good science in what John says and does. He does things this way almost instinctively and because he has a long history of asking for feedback and acting on it. Those who know behavior analysis can see how it informs all of his actions. Learn the science and review what John does so you can have the same impact he is able to accomplish during challenging times.

What I Like about John's Story

- He earns trust by consistently nurturing it. If he has critical information he would say, "I do have the information, but I am unable to share it now. I will share the information on ___ day."

- He has a clear line of sight.

- He listens to his people as they strive toward the line of sight.

- He recognizes that his positive leadership matters and he makes frequent attempts to reach out to his people with effective use of *The 3-Minute Meeting*™.

- He looks at the behavior of his followers.

- He encourages people to tell him the truth along the way.

- He follows up.

- He finds out what is working.

- He makes it safe to make mistakes and learn from them.

The Laws of Behavior Affect Us 24/7

I was reviewing some of the principles of behavior analysis with a leader. She said, "This applies to everything. When I try to diet or work out or raise my kids or work on changing organizations, it's all the same stuff." And it is. The real issue isn't one of knowledge or understanding but of application and action. Rapid change requires taking some action immediately rather than learning new information without application.

Let's consider an example from a popular workout program, *P90X*. Successful workout programs are the ones where people report that they try the program, continue to do it over time and doing so results in getting in shape, losing weight and looking and feeling fit. These are programs that work.

P90X: The Value of Brief, Frequent Touch Points

This workout program includes a series of DVDs. They start with a brief prologue and words of encouragement from the primary trainer, Tony Horton. He makes some brief comments before the video fades to one of his catchphrases—"Bring It!"

Tony usually has three or four other relatively fit individuals behind him on the video. Different levels of workout difficulty are typically displayed by Tony's workout partners. Usually one of the trainers is advanced, another is exercising at a moderate difficulty and a third person is at a beginner's level.

Tony may share a suggestion for the day like "Remember to breathe" or "Clear your mind" that he repeats a few times during the workout.

The workout consists of a series of exercises repeated up to three or more times. Small and frequent breaks are built in. You are encouraged to try it and make small adjustments to your own workout. You are reminded to have specific goals and to write down what you did after each set.

He demonstrates the exercise and then checks on the other trainers. He frequently comments on what they are doing that is correct and this serves to reinforce what *good* looks like. Tony also shows the slight variations of doing the exercises that are within acceptable range. He makes small adjustments and corrections. He doesn't require rigid adherence to his program but encourages individuals to modify the workout to fit their individual needs.

The behaviors of the trainers and leader are essential to the success of this and many current workout programs. When these behaviors are transferred to you, then you have a good chance of experiencing sustainable change. Let's look at all the little things that occur during this program that help to make it work.

What I Like about Tony's Training

- Tony makes it fun. He isn't focused on getting

it perfect. He is interested in getting action started and fine-tuning it once it is happening. He is often heard saying, "Do your best and forget the rest."

- He focuses on making small adjustments during the activity. If the exercise is too difficult or a weight is too heavy, he is able to point out a way to modify it to make it work for you.

- He focuses on daily action. The focus is on working the program on a daily basis. It is difficult to build new habits when you are not doing something daily or at least multiple times during the week.

- He focuses on repetition. This helps to create new habits and build fluency.

- He uses goal setting. He asks multiple times during each workout how many reps the other trainers have set for each exercise.

- He encourages self-monitoring. He asks people where they are in their own counting by asking "How many is that?" He also asks them to write down their progress after each exercise.

- He makes it easy to get started, to keep going and to finish. Do something first then modify how it works.

- Tony's approach addresses performers at all levels, from beginner to advanced, and he provides slight variations that allow people to make the exercises work for them.

Self-Change for Leaders—Jackie's Story

Many of the best leaders and coaches of change I have worked with are their own toughest critics. Jackie exemplifies this point. I first met Jackie during a workshop. She had been to many similar training events before in her career but despite that she took good notes, paid attention and was eager to learn. The first session she had was on developing change plans for her direct reports. The leader of this team wanted each manager to develop two change plans during that session.

This was the kind of session that I usually don't enjoy conducting. It lasted four hours and the follow-up, by the leader's choice, was left to chance—not usually the best way to leave a lasting impression. This situation was unique since I was working with Jackie who was skilled at effective implementation and follow-up. I saw Jackie again a year later. She was telling someone else I was working with at that time about the training that she went to and what she wanted to do next with it. She started to describe the session in great detail. That wasn't the uncanny part of the conversation. Jackie started to describe very quickly five or six change plans that she had developed over the last 12 months. She developed two during the session and then went on to develop others on her own after the session. The plans took care and time to develop. She also had success with all or most of the plans.

The truly impressive thing is that she was able to describe the pinpoints she had developed for three or four of her plans. As Jackie was describing her plans to me, I think my jaw dropped because she stopped talking and asked, "What?" She said I was looking at her with my mouth wide open and she wanted to know why. This says something about what a good observer Jackie is. I told her that I was impressed at the level of specific detail in her plans that she had developed largely on her own with her direct reports. I was surprised since she only attended a four-hour session and I have seen people attend a week's worth of training with six months of follow-up support who were still unable to do what she was doing. She smiled and maybe deflected some of my compliments. Since I couldn't help myself, I asked her, "How did you do that?"

Here's what Jackie said:

> I took good notes and developed a good draft during the session. Then I met with the people I wrote the plans for and we modified the plans together. I gave them leeway to make the plans their own. I asked them a few questions as we fine-tuned the plans and ensured that they were our plans, not my plans. I also applied what we covered in the session. The things that worked,

I kept doing. The things that didn't, I modified. I also built in small, frequent touch points for the people I was working with. Every week or so, I evaluated what was working and then repeated that. I would then pick one to two things to modify each week so that I was able to continue to improve. This is what I did to not only develop plans for my people, but to also use the plans to help them get better.

What I Like about Jackie's Story

This brief story includes several best practices that are worth highlighting.

- Jackie, one of the top coaches I have ever worked with, is always looking for one to two things to improve in her own behavior. She may know more than most people about coaching, but she is always eager to learn one more thing to make her an even better coach.

- She didn't assume that the plan developed on the first day was the end-point of her work. She not only developed draft plans, she then worked the plans to make them better and to ensure they helped. She worked these plans with persistent, consistent and helpful touch points.

- She transferred her learning to different situations after she got better at plan development.

Notably, Jackie is also successful at finding ways to fit working out into her days and weeks. She works hard at her job and works long hours, yet she is able to find time to run, even if that means getting up at 4 a.m. to stay healthy. This change stuff, whether it is working out or coaching your people, may not be complicated but it isn't always easy. It is much easier to sleep in than to get up at the wee hours of the morning. It is much easier to develop a batch of plans, hand out the instructions and blame your people six months later when nothing has changed. In Jackie's case, she is willing to not just start strong, but do the daily things, like providing frequent touch points or working out each day, that will help her pull through the changes she desires.

Continuing to review examples like these will assist you in identifying the specific behaviors that help leaders get change to stick and will help in illustrating the principles at work. The principles of rapid change were at work in this chapter's examples whether they were readily apparent or not. John is a leader who is very skilled at maintaining a clear line of sight and encouraging people to take action and do something even during tough times. Tony's story emphasizes doing something today and practicing with repetition. Jackie is one of the best at breaking behaviors into component parts and fine-tuning along the way.

SECTION II

PATH TO RAPID CHANGE

This section deals with the path from getting change started, to making it work, to getting it to stick. It includes details that will help leaders and managers influence change in a positive way and build a culture where individuals are working at optimal levels not because they have to but because they want to. This section also includes details on how you can incrementally build the science of change into your approach as well as how to overcome the inevitable signs of resistance that you will encounter along the way.

CHAPTER 5

THE PATH

To understand the kind of change that is possible for any type of effort, it is helpful to get a sense of how performance varies over time. The research on performance potential includes a concept called *discretionary effort*. This concept illustrates how to accelerate and optimize change. It also provides a path from not doing something at all, to getting started, to making it work at the highest levels. Discretionary effort is about optimizing performance and ensuring the changes stick.

Discretionary Effort—The Path of Change

The discretionary effort graphic on the next page provides a summary of research on human performance. It also describes a path to long-term sustainable positive change. Let's walk through the graphic. The graphic shows performance, which is a combination of results and behaviors, on one axis and time along the other axis.

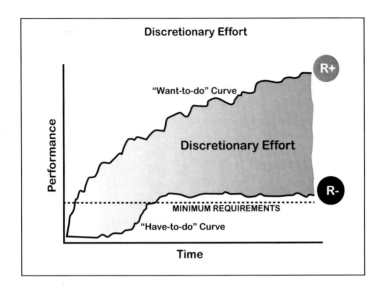

The dotted line represents the minimum performance levels. It represents compliance. Some individuals hover at this level and stay there. They give exactly what is asked for—no more, no less. They are checking the box and doing just enough to remain employed. The idea is to do what is minimally required and save some energy and effort for other things that they'd rather be doing, like surfing the Internet or going home early. Individuals operate at this level not because they *want to* but because they *have to.* They have to in order to fly below the radar, avoid detection, and avoid getting caught. Behavioral research indicates that this level of performance is created through something called *negative reinforcement,* an often misunderstood psychological concept.

Negative reinforcement is doing something to avoid an undesirable consequence like getting fired or getting in trouble. It is an outcome of managing by exception. If you only manage exceptions, you are leaving performance on the table and are not anywhere near attaining even average performance. In the workplace, if someone says, "I only hear from my boss when there is a problem" they are likely being managed primarily through negative reinforcement. The issue then becomes that people perform to avoid hearing from the boss, being found out, being an outlier and so on. Negative reinforcement creates a fairly specific performance function—individuals perform just at or slightly above the minimum performance expectations. They do what they do because they "have to" in order to avoid being detected.

Compliance is not really as simple as this line hovering above minimum performance. Individuals perform at this level only when someone is looking. When no one is looking, who knows what is actually happening? Individuals in this kind of situation may only reach that compliance level when they believe someone is checking. When no one is observing or checking, the behavior is unlikely to occur. In other words, they go back to surfing the Internet, playing solitaire, checking their Smart phones or gossiping with a coworker.

Negative reinforcement is also a hallmark of reactive approaches to work and to management. If managers speak to their employees only when there is a problem, they are likely to create the kind of performance function seen at the compliance line. Bosses may also skip over or ignore all of the good work that is occurring. This is common when people get really busy—"I am too busy to focus on the new changes we were supposed to focus on so I may speak to my employees or the team only when there is a problem. When there is a problem or an issue, we work hard to resolve it." In these conditions employees see what happens over time. The boss only engages people when there is a problem, crisis or issue. Employees then work hard to ensure they are not a problem. In these conditions employees avoid telling the boss the truth. They hide bad news. They also avoid approaching the boss. If managers focus only on the poor or bad examples, problems, crises, or issues, they will not create optimal performance—*discretionary effort.*

Negative reinforcement has its place. The appropriate use of negative reinforcement by managers to motivate others is when they want only compliance or to get behavior started. Negative reinforcement may also be an effective strategy when any of us drift off of our predetermined path or when dealing with true fires and crises. There are times when "Get it done or else" is needed. Real fires and crises exist. Patterns of fighting fires, however, may indicate that negative reinforcement is the primary approach to management rather than a deliberate choice to deal with this crisis now because it requires this kind of response.

Some kinds of changes and behaviors just need to occur. A common example is expense reporting. Expense reports need to be accurate and completed by a certain deadline, but individuals are unlikely to get extra credit for doing them early. For most jobs, expense reporting is a required part of the job but not the central part of the job, so knowing there will be repercussions if you miss the deadline is the driver or negative reinforcer. The qualifier "negative" is neither bad nor good. It means that behavior is prompted to avoid something perceived to be undesirable (i.e., negative).

Compliance plays a role in change efforts, but it should not occupy the central role. Negative reinforcement creates a "have to do" culture and does not create a "want to do" culture where people do what they are supposed to do even when no one is looking.

The desired path leads to optimal performance—the do-more-than-I-have-to-do-when-necessary performance defines discretionary effort. The gap between minimum performance and optimal performance *requires* discretionary effort. This kind of performance function can only be created by a particular kind of reinforcement—the effective use of positive reinforcement.

Positive reinforcement, like negative reinforcement, is a widely misunderstood concept. In its simplest form it is anything that increases the future likelihood of something occurring again. It is something perceived to be desirable. Most individuals think about it as money and recognition. These are potential examples of positive reinforcement but they are not the most important ones for getting change to work or be sustained. Understanding the kinds of positive reinforcers (other than rewards and recognition) that really influence optimal performance is the key to bringing about change that works and sticks.

Let's review top performers or individuals who operate at a high-and-steady rate of performance. Two questions should be asked here—"Where do top performers get their reinforcement?" and "Who provides reinforcement for them?" The first answer I hear usually is that top performers receive reinforcement from themselves. Top performers reinforce their own exceptional behavior. They know what a good job looks like today. When they drive home at the end of the workday, their self-assessment of the job they did serves to reinforce some of their habits that have a desired impact on the work and the customer, and that will eventually lead to solid results.

Top performers also receive reinforcement on a daily basis from the group they are likely to spend most of their time with—their customers. If you compare the amount of time top performers (in certain jobs, of course) spend with their boss versus their internal or external customers, they resoundingly spend more time with their customers. After self-assessment, customers are the greatest source of reinforcement in the workplace for all performers.

Two other sources of reinforcement are worth discussing—reinforcement from the work itself and from peers. With top performers, both the work itself and peers may affect their performance on a daily or weekly basis. Consider top performers and what they talk about at the end of the day. Have you ever heard a top performer in any field talk about the work itself or the game or the sale? This kind of detail is important to them. They may have taken additional steps that others chose not to take. Peers in many jobs are around more frequently than managers or leaders. Individuals may appreciate feedback from peers more than bosses because peers really know what's happening and they are usually around more often. Any change initiative that does not take into account one or more of the following sources of consequences—self, customers, the work and peers—is unlikely to have long-term sustainable impact.

The highest level of performance is worth exploring since it provides a target for the desired state—high levels of performance. Individuals do what they do because they want to and the behaviors they are demonstrating are at habit strength. Habit strength is important when attempting to ensure sustained change. It is doing something at a high-and-steady rate and in a way that is automatic. Habit strength is sometimes referred to as *unconscious competence.*

When attempting to bring about change that sticks, it is helpful to design a pathway that provides guidance incrementally over time to habit strength and optimal levels of performance. The issue is that when trying new and different things, these attempts aren't reinforced by us, customers, the work or peers. In fact, the natural reaction to an unmanaged attempt is more likely to stop, block, or interfere with the desired change. Individuals may personally think the new or different thing is too hard to do or too much work. Customers may react negatively when employees try new things since they may be awkward with their first attempts. Peers may tell each other point blank to stop trying the new thing since inadvertently some peers may be making others who aren't participating look bad. And the work itself may not feel easy or comfortable. During this period, the manager's role is to bridge the gap with reinforcement that encourages people to continue the new or different behaviors.

A proactive influencer role in this period is essential. The manager's job is to reinforce early and often. Money and recognition alone will not work here. The role is not to reinforce with just pats on the back and saying "good job" over and over again. Consider the four consequences that matter—self, customers, the work and peers.

The manager's job in the early phases of a change effort is to ask questions to connect the performer to the consequences that matter. Ask others to describe how it worked. This prompts self-evaluation and self-reinforcement when it is a good experience. Ask others to describe something that they learned. This could help them see the value and reinforcement in the new behavior. Ask others about how internal or external customers responded, to help them see that what they did worked or helped with their customers.

If the goal is to systematically set behavior at the level of compliance, then tell people what to do and solve their problems for them. If the goal is to systematically create optimal performance, the behavior of influencers must include asking questions and facilitating change. Questions create self-reinforcement and help individuals see their impact on customers and the work.

Here are a few sample questions to help people who are trying new things to make that change continue and get on the path toward optimal performance.

- How did you do that?

- How did the customer respond?

- What did you think?

- How did that work when you tried it?

- What part of the new or different thing worked better than last time?

Three Phases on the Path to Rapid Change

The path to a culture of discretionary effort includes three phases from getting started, to making it work, to getting it to stick.

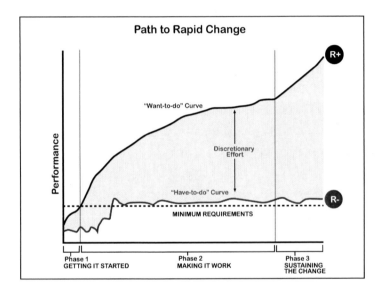

1. Getting Started

When trying to get something started, negative rein-forcement—as defined earlier—may be appropriate. Tell people what you want them to do. Say, "try this" when referring to a new or different thing. It is during this phase that the focus is on the structure or process. Individuals follow the guidelines or checklists in this early phase because it is new or different. Initially, people may only comply. Be less concerned about it working well or getting great at it yet, as those are performance levels which are probably many repetitions away. In this phase, the important thing is to do it once and then make repeated attempts. Our old habits may be in the way. Individuals may not actually agree with or believe in the new initiative. They may not buy in yet. That is fine. You could spend all of your time trying to elaborate on the merits of the new change and arguing with people so that they buy in. Or you can encourage action and then help others see or experience the benefits of the desired changes. If you only want compliance, then stop here. If you want more than compliance and if you want people to do the new or different thing when no one is looking, then shift to the next phase.

2. Making It Work

This is a challenging phase for many individuals and organizations, but it is the one to master to attain sustainable change. Most individuals have considerable experience with the *getting started phase* and in spending too much time stalled in that phase. Moving out of the *getting started phase* is essential if real change is desired. When attempting to make it work, it is not adequate to just try it. Here the focus is on trying to make it work. In the *getting started phase*, individuals may try something that feels uncomfortable and doesn't work. During the *making it work phase,* small changes to what you are doing are needed to improve the effectiveness of the change.

The role of leadership here is to ask more and tell less. Telling was appropriate in the *getting started phase*. In this next phase, coaching rather than training is the effective behavior of those trying to help and trying to bring about change. Facilitating answers rather than solving problems for others also helps us move beyond compliance.

In the *getting started phase* you need to see behavior occur. In the *making it work phase* you are trying to find effectiveness in what people are doing. In the *getting it to stick phase* the shift is to finding efficiencies and creating good habits.

3. Getting It to Stick

The *getting it to stick phase* includes reaching habit strength in the behaviors and desired impact in the results. It includes a high degree of self-management by performers. It requires less involvement by management and leadership. The leaders in this phase can help the most by asking questions and facilitating change rather than telling people what to do. Help by encouraging people to continue to own the changes and by guiding them to their own answers. During this phase there is very little training and telling, some coaching, and a higher degree of facilitation and discovery of best practices by finding out what top performers are doing to make small changes in their own behavior.

In this phase it is necessary to introduce novelty to help make the work fresh and keep the changes going.

Novelty is an important element in this phase since it helps to refocus and re-energize the change effort by introducing small changes that make it more interesting or fun for those engaged in it.

Behavioral Science Helps

Behavioral scientists employ a model to describe and analyze why people do what they do and why they don't always do what they are told to do. This model also helps modify what is happening today and to ensure not only that change occurs, but that it also sticks.

The ABC Model

The ABC Model is used to highlight what influences behavior change. The B stands for Behavior. The two forces that influence behavior are A for Antecedents and C for Consequences. Antecedents come before behavior and get it started. Consequences are anything that happens during and after the behavior that encourages, discourages or stops the behavior altogether.

Antecedents prompt the occurrence of behaviors but have a limited role in keeping behavior going. Common antecedents include telling people what to do, plans, getting buy-in, training, policies, procedures, goals, objectives, processes and job aids. Consequences include both positive and negative consequences. Consequences occur during and after the behavior and have by far the greatest influence over future occurrences of behavior.

To get behavior started, antecedents provide good options. But when the desired outcome is behavior continuing over time and becoming a habit, the right consequences are needed. There are many kinds of consequences, as discussed previously, like money and pats on the back, but the ones that are most powerful are *immediate* and *certain*. The *during* consequences are a rich source of ensuring change such as consequences and reinforcement from self, customers, the work and our peers.

Remember that antecedents play a predominant role in the *getting started phase*. Consequences are essential to understand and use during the *making it work* and *getting it to stick phases*. Approaching these later phases by only using antecedents—like training, telling, reminding, reviewing the policies, focusing on buy-in, procedures and processes, and creating job aids—will not lead to sustainable change.

The sections that follow include details of each phase of change along the path to rapid change. Each phase should have clear outcomes and a line of sight. Each phase will also require different actions for getting behavior started, making it work, and getting it to stick.

CHAPTER 6

GETTING STARTED

You may have a history of false starts, high hopes, getting stalled, getting stuck, selling people on the change, pushing for buy-in and hearing complaints about why something won't work. This chapter includes details on how to start in an effective way. Options for avoiding some of the traps and ways to increase the chances of moving to the next phase are reviewed.

The point is that you must prepare carefully for getting change started. How can you personally set yourself up for success when you are attempting to create change? How can you help someone else through a change issue or initiative?

An Overview of Getting Started

The first phase of any change initiative is getting started. Those who eventually get change to stick do some specific things well during the *getting started phase.* They also avoid many of the perils of getting started.

Getting started well requires balance. It begins by clearly describing the long-term outcomes, end state and line of sight. It requires starting something today or this week. It requires not being too ambitious. If you plan on doing 30 things, good luck. That may not be practical when you have other work to do like checking your e-mail or voice mail or managing a crisis. Focus on a commitment to one or two things. Try to pick something that is likely to have an impact on your business results. Be able to identify a few early signs that these efforts are working. I'm not talking about the home runs and the big wins here. What are some reasonable early outcomes that would indicate you are on the right track? Repetition helps here too. Don't just pick something you will do once a quarter. This is too infrequent to get good at it.

A quick test—How long will it take you to get great at shooting free throws if you reserve one, eight-hour session per month for practice? It will take forever. How about splitting up that time and doing something every day or every week that can help you get the most repetitions over time?

Try to keep change simple, easy and fun. Try not to make it too complicated and don't expect perfection. Set high standards but just for a few, incremental things. The goal is to attempt the new behavior once and then to make repeated attempts. Avoid expectations of perfection. Trying to do something perfectly could make it too difficult or complicated or serious. Vince Lombardi said, "Practice doesn't make perfect.

Perfect practice makes perfect." But if Vince were coaching a team of newcomers to football, he would have a bunch of frustrated kids. It may take years and many repetitions to be perfect. Practice something that is good enough and that includes what is close to the desired behavior. The caveat, and this will be addressed in the next chapter, is to quickly shift to assessing how the new behavior is working. Keep doing what works and modify what does not. It helps here to have a coach who can talk to you about what happened and offer a few suggestions to tweak what you are doing as you strive for perfect practice over time.

Another caveat here is that bad habits emerge when repeating undesired behaviors over and over again. An example is taking batting practice when you are in a hitting slump. You may reinforce the bad habits without some kind of intervention. The path to change should have some corrections built in to continue to make it work. Doing something that doesn't work over and over again will create or perpetuate bad habits. Keep in mind the definition of *insanity* often attributed to Albert Einstein, which is, "doing the same thing over and over again and expecting different results."

During the *getting started phase* you are essentially establishing the minimum requirements. Get these in place early. Patience for long-term results is required here—deliberate, persistent impatience is reserved for trying new behaviors now. Follow the structure and avoid the temptation to build in shortcuts too soon. As mentioned earlier, "Try it, you'll like it." Well, maybe you won't like it, but you have to try it once to at least see how it might work.

Behavioral Science Helps

Five elements of the science are reviewed here—Antecedents, Negative Reinforcement, Planning and Sequencing Change, Working Backward and the Role of Feedback.

1. Antecedents—Policies, Training and Telling

It is during the early phase that antecedents play the central role. It is here that telling people what to do is appropriate. Be sure to tell people to do the things to help them follow up and arrange the necessary consequences to support the desired changes. This will help transition to the next phase. Antecedents are appropriate for "can't do" problems. A simple test here is to ask this question—can individuals do what they are asked to do if their lives depend on it? If the answer is no, then antecedents are essential. They can't yet do the new behavior unless someone tells them, trains them, or shows them the new process, procedure or tool. Ensure people know what to do and how to do it. It may be that they know how, but other consequences may need to be put in place. Having clear antecedents in the beginning allows a shift in focus to other consequences to get the change started.

2. Negative Reinforcement—Managing Exceptions and Compliance

During this phase identify who will do what. This includes the specific actions and behaviors of employees, managers and leaders. Clarify expectations and identify requirements for every level. Prompt everyone to begin the desired change. Encourage individuals to start. Many will start to avoid being the exception and to meet the minimum requirements. Others become exceptions to manage.

3. Planning and Sequencing Change

Devise a brief, "good enough" plan to get started. Identify behaviors that will have early impact and pick one to two behaviors to focus on now. The other ones that are also important can be our focus later.

4. Working Backward

Continue to keep the end in mind as you talk about the intentions of the change. Identify clearly what you want. This will help us determine if the impact of our initial plan moves in the right direction. It will also help—through reverse engineering or working backward—identify the right behaviors that can provide guidance to this end point. When working backward (see Chapter 3), be sure to link the actions and behaviors to specific results.

5. The Role of Feedback and Reinforcement

Feedback should be used to encourage individuals who are making attempts to get started. Reinforce these attempts early and often. Feedback can be used to emphasize the good examples when individuals get started. Emphasize the behaviors that worked to build a bridge to the *making it work phase*. Feedback can also be used to encourage others who haven't made any attempts to get started.

Suggestions for Getting Started

The role of leaders early on is to encourage people to try it. Look for good examples of attempts. Ask people to describe what is working. Resist the temptation to drill down on all the things that aren't working too early. In the *getting started phase,* encourage attempts early and often. Provide the extra time to those who are trying the new behaviors. Offer suggestions that help and that are likely to work rather than making suggestions that add a lot more work for others.

1. Try It.

"Just Do It" is a great slogan for selling sneakers and an apt phrase when getting started with a new initiative. If "do it" works, then great. When "do it" doesn't work, other options are needed. "Try it or try it today." If you have a choice to debate someone for an hour about the merits of the new thing or if you can encourage them to try it and then talk about how it worked, I'd recommend trying it and then talking about it afterward. Resist the long debate over whether it works and get down to some action today. Some approaches to change related to treatment for addiction or dieting discourage the use of a phrase like "try it" since it implies "I might do it, but I probably won't." This is important especially when considering your internal dialogue. If someone is thinking "I might do that" or "I'll try that," it is not as certain as "I'll do that now." That's not the issue here since the point is about influencing others not yourself. "Try it right now" is a great reply to someone who wants to talk about all the reasons why something won't work. Try it now and then let's talk about what happened when you tried it. What part of it worked? What part felt comfortable? What kind of value did you see when you tried it? The phrase "do it" might lead to "but it won't work." My reply is, "You might be right. Try it now and we'll have something to talk about after. You might prove me wrong. I'm betting that you'll be able to see it work." As my friend Linda, who is a great coach and manager, would say, "Try it. There's no telling what we're going to learn."

2. I Have a Suggestion . . .

"Constructive feedback" gets a bad rap, although that bad rap is often earned because of poor delivery. When someone asks, "Can I give you some feedback?" it usually is a sign that the feedback isn't going to have a positive tone. To shape incremental changes today, feedback should include what you liked, not because you are attempting to be merely positive, but to ensure that a desired behavior is repeated. Feedback that is reinforcing may have constructive elements when it starts with "I have a suggestion." Constructive feedback has a path forward; negative feedback does not. This may be especially true when I hear a suggestion, try it, and see good things happen when I put the suggestion into practice. A suggestion that is tried right away and that works is reinforcing when it works. Some of the burden then is on the person who is offering suggestions. Try to describe your suggestions in a way that is likely to work right away. If someone tried something and you noted 50 things that you didn't like, resist the temptation to blurt out all those things. Instead, consider one or two actions that this person can try right now, that they can see work when they take your advice. When suggestions are offered and individuals try them, it indicates movement out of the *getting started phase,* and into the *making it work phase.*

3. Good Examples are Good for Business.

When focusing on what is not working, you learn what not to do. I don't know about you, but I get paid for doing something, not for avoiding something. When your energy and attention are focused on all the things that aren't working, you delay building new behaviors and skills. When focusing on the good examples, you can then repeat or replicate what worked, as long as you consider what was done that led to the good example. Reviewing the good examples also provides specific details about what you need to do more of, that you can build upon.

4. This is a Good Time for Making a Great Speech.

One of the best times for a good speech is when you are attempting to get change started. Such speeches often describe where you are and where you are going. The speech may include the case for change and what everyone needs to do to get there. It may ask for individual commitments. However, if leaders continue only with good speeches—which are antecedents—without follow-up in the later stages, then they are likely to fall into the cycle of starting a lot of changes but finishing few of them. Behavior needs consequences, especially specific follow-up. It also needs clear signals of its value to increase its occurrence.

Six Challenges to Getting Started

When you are first approaching the *getting started phase* you may hear others say things that could stall the change or get it off track in a hurry. You may hear these things from others but you also may be saying some of these things yourself. The simplest answer to many challenging statements is a version of the "try it" suggestion.

Six Challenges to Getting Started

1.	I already do that.
2.	Great stuff. I need to know more.
3.	I first need the buy-in of everyone involved.
4.	This won't work.
5.	I'll try that later.
6.	The organization needs to…

1. I already do that.

This is one of the common statements heard at the beginning of a change initiative. Is it true? Maybe. It may be that the person or group already does the desired change. What I usually hear at the beginning of a change initiative is a select group who will say "I already do that." What they are really saying is, "I am not going to try it." "I already do that" is often a red flag signaling that nothing new will be tried. The antidote to "I already do that" is "Then how will you fine-tune what you already do so that you do it better?" or "What will you try that will refine part of what you are already doing?" The point here is to shift focus away from attempts to try nothing new to attempts to try something new. It is impossible to see something work when you won't even try it once.

2. Great stuff. I need to know more.

Beware the flood of questions and attempts to over prepare. These could be genuine signs of interest and enthusiasm, but they may also be a stall tactic. Spending all of the time gathering more information, trying to get it just right, needing to know a lot more than they know now, trying to be perfect when they do something the first time, waiting for exactly the right time and so on—all of these activities delay getting started. Look at what is done rather than what is said. You may easily mistake all these responses for extreme interest. Let's look instead to what action is taking place. What actually was tried and what actually happened?

I once worked with a leader who developed a change plan during the launch of an initiative. He then wanted to gather more information about how it all started, conduct research and analysis, gather information from each of his people and have conversations regarding what everyone thought and felt about it. It was a lot of preliminary work. He sent me drafts of his plans over a period of several months. About three months later he felt like he had it exactly right and then half his team members changed and he was back to the drawing board. It would take him another few months to get the revised plan back on track and before you know it, the organization lost interest and he didn't have to do it anymore.

3. I first need the buy-in of everyone who will be involved.

Buy-in is overrated. Organizations and leaders often spend too much time trying to ensure that others buy in to a change effort. Consider a pie chart that represents buy-in from 100 percent of the workforce. A certain percentage will buy in right in the beginning. Think about this group as early adopters. They will say they are willing to try something. They are enthusiastic. They listen to what leadership is saying and they agree to give it a shot. Take this buy-in and enjoy it. This is the population that you will return to when you are looking for good examples of what happens when people try the new thing.

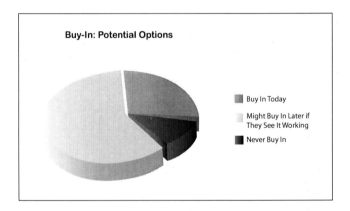

There is another percentage—usually a small one—that will never buy in. All the usual clichés apply here like "when hell freezes over" or "when pigs fly." Be careful not to reinforce this group for their lack of buy-in and for their complaints. **Don't take the bait.** This group may waste valuable time holding discussions about all the reasons why the change effort is a bad idea. They may share this information with leadership, peers or even their direct reports. In the beginning, briefly listen to them to show empathy. Initially listen to them because they may have some ideas worth listening to. At some point you may be reinforcing complaining rather than individuals doing their jobs. They may spend more time talking about why things won't work than it takes to actually try the new thing. I'd set this group aside for the moment. This group, especially in the beginning, will not help get change started.

A third group, and a group that is likely the largest percentage in the pie chart, is the group that doesn't buy in today but will buy in later if they start to see the change initiative working and see promising signs that this time will be different. This is the group that can help the most in any change initiative. This is the group that you encourage to try it and help them see how it is working so that they continue to try it. Converting this group to the next phase in the change process is a primary objective when getting change to work and stick.

Is buy-in *necessary* to get started? Not really. If I can get buy-in, I will take it. But when you don't have buy-in, merely getting people to tell you what you want to hear, will likely get verbal behavior—people saying the right things, rather than actual behavior change—people *demonstrating* desired behaviors. A side effect of pushing for too much buy-in is that individuals may just tell leadership what it wants to hear. The reasoning is,

"I'll say the right things, but I'm just going to wait it out. The new thing usually goes away eventually anyway." If the desired change is people saying how important the new change is and if that is all you want, then go for it. Push for buy-in. But if you want changes in how the work is done, in customer responses and business results, you will need to see changes in your behavior and that of your employees. What kind of buy-in is really needed? The only buy-in you need is people willing to try it for a period of time.

Another note about hearing what is on people's minds— some of the strongest advocates over time are sometimes the individuals who, in the beginning, were the most vocal in their objection to the change. These individuals in their initial opposition may actually be expressing how much they care about what they do.

I worked in a call center years ago that had been through no fewer than 30 change initiatives in 30 years. This group was very suspicious of change and of false promises that this time it would be different. The typical change effort started off with a big splash and a speech by the leader. About six months later that same leader was making a big splash and a speech for a different change initiative. So this time there were no grand announcements. Instead the focus was on making the change work and to be seen as helpful. The goal was to make sure that supervisors and managers actually helped their direct reports through effective coaching and development. The culture was punishing and was challenging to work in. Supervisors initially just fought fires and only approached employees when things were off track.

Instead of promising that it would be different, the focus was demonstrating that it could work differently. It took about three to four months for this shift to occur. Near the end of that period, I was waiting for an elevator and an employee was waiting there with me. She said that she'd seen me around the center and wondered what I was doing with the managers and supervisors. I was surprised that she asked me such a direct question. I asked her what she meant and she said that she didn't know what I was doing but if it had anything to do with the fact that the supervisors were finally doing their jobs and managing in an effective way, then keep doing it. "It's about time they finally did their jobs well," she commented. Talk is cheap. Actual change matters. Skipping the promises and speeches at this facility and focusing instead on observable change led to the desired outcomes.

4. This won't work.
The truth is that the change might not work. When people say at the beginning that it won't work, they may be on to something. But when they say this and aren't willing to even try the new or different thing, they aren't going to have success. The challenge for leaders is to encourage people to say what they really think but to also balance that with ensuring that people

will attempt the change.

5. I'll try that later.

When someone agrees to try something later, this too may be an honest answer. A follow-up question would be, "When?" If later is always tomorrow, you won't have much success. Encourage individuals to share details about when they might try something. Encourage them to share how it worked as soon as they try it. A question my friend James would ask is, "Why do we wait?"

6. The organization needs to fix compensation . . . offer more support . . . provide more resources . . . others need to do something first . . . quick, look over there . . . blah, blah, blah . . .

Many things are beyond our control. The behavior of others and larger organizational changes may put you in a position to wait. When you wait, you are static— not changing. Some changes will take time. Other changes you may want now but what will you do or try when those other changes are not yet in place? Do you really need to fix everything else first, before taking action? The antidote is a familiar one. All of these changes would be great. If other people do some of the things you want them to do, that certainly will help. But if you approach this by only waiting, nothing will change. Encourage individuals to focus on what is controllable—their own behavior. What can they try and do, that works and helps? What is within their control? Let's figure that out and do it.

Blocking and Tackling—Don's Story

Don worked for Mike. (See Mike's story in Chapter 2.) Don was a no-nonsense guy from the Pittsburgh area who was assigned the task of turning around a call center of about 700 people. I'd seen two other talented leaders try and fail to turn this place around and the smart money would be that Don too would fail. Don was different though. He could smell bull miles away and had very high expectations, but he was the kind of leader who was not afraid of the work and not afraid to get his hands dirty . . . and Don had *a lot* of work to do.

He started by setting up a giant board with the names and pictures of every employee in his organization. He did this for a few reasons. A primary reason was that he needed help in bringing about this change. It also showed that Don was willing to be out in the workplace with his people. This was the first step he took within this center. He wanted to observe. He wanted to get to know people. He wanted to show the entire workforce that he was able to see things with his own eyes and listen to what people were saying. Over time it became a way for him to follow up and check on how things went with issues he heard about on previous days. Don got to know his people. He showed them he could listen rather than talk at them. He observed and learned what they did that worked well. Actually there was plenty that did work well. He also learned on his own through observing and asking people about what didn't work. He used this information to hold people accountable and he expected all of his managers and leaders to not just know the names of people, but to be out of their cubicles and offices observing the work, being available and helping their people on a daily basis—not just when things weren't working but when they were.

Don also knew that he wasn't going to turn things around on his own. He needed to identify—not by hearsay but by what he observed—who the people were who could help him get to the future state that he wanted for the center. He knew how to create an organization that had clear expectations of performance and how to then follow up on these expectations with consistency and persistence.

Frequency and Follow-Up Count

Don was part of a team that identified the kinds of things they as leaders could put into place that would accelerate the rate of change. They wanted employees to not just have lengthy plans on what they were going to do, but lots of brief plans that guided frequent coaching and influenced touch points. Don recognized that in order to change faster, he needed a clear breakdown of what they wanted the frontline employees to do. They also needed to help managers and coaches build behavior change faster through repetition in specific and proactive coaching behaviors. They weren't going to sit back in their nice offices and have formal meetings once a month with each employee. At the very least they were going to have more, shorter but impactful, positive touch points for each coach in the organization. This wasn't managing by walking around. This was observing what was happening and identifying what worked early and often. It was providing feedback that helped.

Earn the Right to Coach

Don and his team of leaders started with the recommendations on how to increase their touch points, which are those brief, helpful coaching interactions that are essential for supporting incremental change. The goal of the touch points was to help bring about change more quickly—the desired changes in frontline employee behaviors, observed changes in customer responses and positive changes in business results. Initially the team started with more daily and weekly touch points. Don and his team used to joke that they were able to bring about changes per hour which were later accelerated to changes per minute. This required skill in behavior change and shaping, which his team practiced and refined on a daily basis.

Don and his leaders found ways to infuse the workplace with more helpful positive touch points not just by observing but by doing something with the observations. The leaders asked more and better questions, found quicker ways to give feedback and get to the point, and discovered different ways to give feedback in the moment. Even when frontline employees were on the phone with customers, leaders wrote quick notes or pointed to something on the computer screen. Many of the employees wanted the managers around during this period because these managers actually helped. They offered suggestions that worked. They provided real-time suggestions that improved specific calls. They also offered coaching that wasn't designed to take over the call but to help the frontline employees do it on their own.

I watched one encounter where the supervisor was observing and guiding the frontline employee along the way. The supervisors may have taken over some complicated calls in the past and employees may have been glad to let them do so. However, this time the coach offered guidance along the way and helped the employee do it on her own. At the end of the call the employee said, "I didn't think I could handle that kind of call. You proved to me today that I could do it on my own if I just tried to make a few small changes in my approach. I think I could handle that situation on my own in the future."

Begin with Accountability and Transparency

Don was asked to kick off a training class on active listening within his large call center. Two of his direct reports were facilitating it because he wanted to establish ownership of the follow-up and the content within his leadership team, rather than within the training department. Don kicked off the session with the following words:

> I'd like to share four things with you today as you start on this training. Number one, have fun. You're here anyway; you might as well enjoy this experience. Number two, be open to learn new things. You may know some of this but there is something in this for every one of us. Number three, make a commitment to practice the new skills today and when you get back to the floor. It's not about just learning something new; it's about putting it into practice.

Don then asked everyone there if they were willing to make those commitments. Everyone nodded. And then Don said the following:

> Good, I am glad you are all committed to trying this. The fourth thing I want to share with you is that tomorrow I will be listening to your calls because I'd like to hear how different your calls will be based on this training.

Several jaws dropped, because they knew Don. He does what he says he will do, so they knew they'd better give this stuff a fair shot.

Later, Don reflected on why he chose to take this approach, and here's what he said:

> The biggest thing missing in most leaders is follow-up. Everyone has a plan. Everyone has a goal. Everyone does the analysis and assessment. Everyone puts a problem-solving process in place. Some people measure. Few people follow up and that is the part I want all of my leaders and team members to get good at doing. It is not enough just to send a bunch of people to a training class. Expect to see evidence that the class content will be applied back on the floor. The best way to do that is to follow up. I hold myself accountable for the follow-up and I hold my people accountable to do their part.

Don's follow-up wasn't a "gotcha." He had a history with this group of encouraging and reinforcing employees who applied things on the floor. He also pointed out when people weren't doing what they said they were going to do. If you do that consistently, then you put your people and yourself in a position to reinforce desirable behavior. That was the history that he had created and that was the kind of culture that existed among his team.

Don talked to all of his people often and made clear that a value of the organization would be to tell the truth no matter how ugly it was. He talked about it a lot and encouraged people to share honest, objective and helpful feedback. He spoke regularly to various team members at different levels across the organization. During those brief meetings, he asked a few people to describe the top two or three things they found helpful about how they were being managed. He also asked them to identify one or two things that would help them the most. He usually had to ask this in different ways to encourage the employees to tell the truth but not put their bosses in a tough spot. One pattern emerged when he gathered this feedback. The theme was that his leaders were doing a lot of the right things, but they never took things off people's plates. In some cases, tasks are no longer needed or are not priorities anymore. As a team, they developed a way to address this issue. When you are confronted with something that's in the way, you have three options—change it, continue it, or kill it.

What I Like about Don's Story

Don is effective at getting change started for several reasons.

- He and his team got started right away. They didn't spend weeks and months planning, analyzing and talking.

- He had crystal-clear expectations.

- Each person had a role and they were accountable for doing something daily. Employees had a key job and supervisors and managers also had important proactive work to do.

- He quickly shifted focus of the culture so that supervisors, managers and leaders helped employees on a frequent basis.

- He modeled by asking good questions, helping and keeping daily commitments.

- And of course, he followed up daily, both with what he liked and what he could reinforce and, importantly, he offered a few suggestions that would help others keep things on track.

Leading with persistent, deliberate impatience is essential in the *getting started phase*. Creating conditions where individuals do something different now and where they try it are necessary in this phase. Don started with his line of sight and began to break down key behaviors into their component parts. He is a master at holding people accountable—including himself. He's also someone who is able to get people to try something new and different now.

The *getting started phase* requires some of the traditional tools that build compliance and that get change started quickly. You can greatly enhance the initial kick-off by pulling forward many of the tips in the next section. Be clear on what you want in the *getting started phase* and set reasonable boundaries for the behaviors that constitute trying it so that individuals can be reinforced for their honest attempts at getting started. This will allow them to know what they can do to begin owning the change and enable them to make reasonable modifications to what they're being asked to do.

CHAPTER 7

MAKING IT WORK

Now it's time to go beyond getting started. How can you modify what you are doing so that it works better for you? What small changes can you make that will allow you to continue trying the new behavior or skill? How can you encourage and help others to go beyond compliance to do something that starts to work better over time?

Individuals and organizations typically have extensive experience with getting change started. The compliance that is required is a lot easier than the challenges inherent in making it work. This step requires an understanding of shaping, behavioral changes and fine-tuning.

This step also requires patience for long-term outcomes and results—the line of sight. There will be a moment during this phase that you and others will question the path, progress and the outcomes. Keep in mind that the long-term outcomes are unlikely to be realized at this point. However, progress toward these outcomes should be evident by now in the activities and behaviors—the leading indicators.

An Overview of Making It Work

The second phase of effectively implementing change is *making it work.* This phase introduces the long road ahead and the realization that the results and outcomes will usually take longer than anticipated. It is in this phase that it is easy to lose patience and question the value of the extra effort and persistence. Small changes to what you are doing are required. You will need more than individuals just trying it here. You'll have to find ways to make it work.

Behavioral Science Helps

Five key elements of the science are reviewed here—Shaping, Positive Reinforcement, Consequences that Matter, Refining Your Pinpoints and Your Plan, and Coaching Rather than Training and Telling.

1. Shaping

This phase is really the incremental change phase. You have taken a few small steps and made some progress. Small changes have been made to what you do to increase the chances the changes lead to desired improvements in business results. Shaping behaviors occurs across employees, managers and leaders as well as setting incremental goals in leading and lagging business results. Shaping is not only applied to the how—the behavior. It is also applied to the what—the near-term results and outcomes that line the path toward the desired end-state.

2. Positive Reinforcement

Reinforce early and often. Plans for change begin with negative reinforcement during the *getting started phase*. You start by telling people what to do and then manage the exceptions. But to make it work, focus is required on the outcomes of the attempts. During this phase, reinforce early and often the honest attempts at small changes. Help others see the impact of their attempts in the work with customers and others. This will help them improve how they are assessing and reinforcing their own behavior. Positive reinforcement is the only consequence that can put individuals on the path to discretionary effort.

3. The Consequences that Really Matter

It will be tempting to only use phrases like "good job" or to hand out tangible rewards when considering how to reinforce on an ongoing basis. If only these two approaches are used, you'll soon run out of rewards and make the phrase "good job" empty and overused. It is essential during this phase to shift the focus to the consequences that really matter—self-reinforcement, customer reinforcement and natural consequences. Natural consequences are active when the work is getting easier, better or more rewarding.

4. Refining Your Pinpoints and Your Plan

Discover which initial parts of the plan and pinpoints work well. It is during this phase that the small refinements in pinpointed behaviors make the biggest differences in whether they work well or not. Uncover and share these small changes that make a big difference.

5. Coaching Rather than Training and Telling

During the *getting started phase*, the focus was on training, telling and a host of other antecedents. It is during the *making it work phase*, that coaching really helps. The kinds of questions asked here are essential. Merely telling people what to do is unlikely to lead to things working better. Asking questions and having discussions about what specifically worked and helped is a better course of action. Effective coaching questions include questions related to the consequences that matter:

- Self-reinforcement—how did you think that went?

- Customer reinforcement—what did you learn from the customer?

- Natural consequences—what was easier or quicker to do than the last time?

Nine Suggestions for Making It Work

1.	Don't overcomplicate it.
2.	Remember that repetition still matters.
3.	Always identify behavior + results.
4.	Focus on incremental change, impact and fine-tuning.
5.	Ask questions.
6.	Ask value questions.
7.	Demonstrate implementation competence.
8.	Build a body of evidence and reinforce the right behaviors along the way.
9.	Keep it fun.

1. Don't overcomplicate it.

Look at what you are doing when you try it. Continue to do what works. Make one or two changes that might help. When you make it more complicated than this, you might just give up. Continue to keep it simple. Now it is a matter of sequencing and recognizing when to move on from one or two behaviors to others. Resist making things more complicated in this phase. The goal is to continue to practice the new behaviors or skills. Begin to apply the new behaviors or skills to other situations during this phase.

2. Remember that repetition still matters.

Monthly frequency is likely not frequent enough for

any change. Find out what you can do or try that occurs often—hourly, daily, or weekly. Build in enough repetition to get good at something and to become fluent at it. Repeated attempts are necessary to help you fine-tune what you are doing and to begin to assess the impact of what you are doing.

3. Always identify behavior + results.

Identify early signs of impact. It is not enough to describe what you will do. A poorly designed plan includes behavior without an impact. When you are identifying a new behavior, also identify the early signs of its impact. These signs should emerge when you try these new behaviors now, today or this week. It is not enough to just plan to ask better questions. Also plan the impact of these questions—What do you want people to share when you ask these questions? What would be a sign of success when you ask these questions? If you ask about the status of an infrequent long-term result, like closing a big sale, you are not going to see much success in your questioning since this is unlikely to happen often. But if your goal is to learn something you don't know, then you can see your questions working today. Behaviors should be linked to some progress in outcomes so that they can be reinforced by what happens in the near term. Linking behaviors only to long-term results does not build reinforcement into the occurrence of the behavior. It is likely here that punishment is paired with the behavior. That is, when

I try the new behavior, nothing good happens and extra time, work and effort happen instead.

Behavior matters not only when getting started but when you are trying to make change work. During the *getting started phase,* complying with some minimum requirement is enough. No need to understand all of the details of pinpointing behaviors. But when looking to make small changes to make things work better, you must break down the behaviors into specific component parts. This specificity or pinpointing requires identifying what is working and then identifying the small changes in behavior that can be made that are likely to improve the outcome. Effective refinement then leads to better behavioral pinpoints and results that can be observed in real time.

4. Focus on incremental change, impact and fine-tuning.

Set intermediate goals to help you stay on the path. Know where you are and know where you ultimately want to be. Once you have framed it this way, fill in the gaps with signs of success along the way. Signs of success include what customers, coworkers or peers say. What kinds of evidence indicate progress? Evidence of progress also includes something being done in a way that takes less time, work and effort. It might be that you have more confidence in a work skill. It could be the customer saying yes to a big deal, but it could also be something as simple as a customer agreeing to another meeting.

One leading indicator of change is evidence that the initial plan has been modified to make the change work. This is something individuals can strive to look for when managing their own behavior and it is also something leaders can ask questions about to determine how the change is being owned by others. A sign of compliance is to merely accept the requested change and take no stake in owning how it works. Finding a way to make small changes to make a change effort work better is a sign of ongoing commitment. The evidence of fine-tuning is a residual effect of moving beyond compliance to commitment and the type of ongoing performance that reflects discretionary effort.

5. Ask questions.

When attempting to make change work, it helps to ensure you help others own their behavior and help them make their own decisions. If your goal is to influence someone else, it helps to work through this in a collaborative way. What will you work on together? What can you try to tweak? The influencer doesn't need to have all the answers, but you should have a way to help people reach answers that show they are improving their current approach to make the change effort work better. Simply asking questions is a good way to facilitate this shift. "You have been complying with the initial program or process for a few weeks. What small changes can you make to improve how it works?"

If there are two choices and the person wants to do choice A but the coach favors choice B, ask questions to encourage the person to talk through what might happen. This helps them see the possible consequences of choice A and B. If they still favor choice A, let them try it as long as a potential negative outcome would only be a small failure. If you are dealing with a high probability of major failure, then intervene. When you are dealing with an acceptable, but not optimal outcome, allow the person to learn from experience. In some cases, choice A may work out and surprise you. Then the coach learns something new about change and about the choice one of the employees made.

6. Ask value questions.

A value question is asking for feedback on the value you provide in helping others. First ask this question before attempting to influence others—"What can I do to help?" Then, ask this question after a coaching interaction—"What was helpful about this coaching?" This second question guides and nudges your interactions to ensure you are having the impact you intend to have. It can also be asked at the beginning and at the end of a meeting. A value question helps focus the group ahead of time so that they agree on what they intend to achieve. It also works at the end of those meetings when asking, "How did we do?"

7. Demonstrate implementation competence.

This phase includes moving beyond merely complying with the minimum requirements and proving to yourself and others that you can get change to occur. Here you can demonstrate that not only are you following the minimal expectations but you are also showing your ability to execute and implement meaningful change. Once everyone learns how to get things accomplished, they begin to learn that the skills required here are transferrable to any change. This is especially helpful since so often the outcome or desired state shifts. By then you have learned exactly how to get change to occur. Importantly, you aren't just learning to engage in the behaviors of the change initiative. By learning how to make it work you learn how to bring about change in any forum. The "what" of the change may be altered, but the "how" will push past incremental change to create transformational change.

8. Build a body of evidence and reinforce the right behaviors along the way.

Pressure will begin to mount. This is a good time to review the body of evidence that is being collected along the way. In the early phases, gather evidence of behavior change from managers, employees and customers. Initial early business results may also emerge during this phase.

One caveat is don't push for the lagging business result too soon. Consider one group I worked with who was known for being very results focused. Some individuals identified the best business results, then they created the behavioral details about how they got the results. This was labeled as "Backing into Business Results." People are watching. What if you took a business result that you got through the usual channels and then trumpeted it as a prime example of the new way? You would then lose credibility with the people—most of the frontline employees—who know the real deal. You also reinforce the perception that leadership only wants to hear good news or use some marketing spin. Avoid this. It is better to share a reasonably good example of employee behaviors and reasonably good business outcomes that are a direct result of the new behaviors. Then you build credibility rather than destroy it.

9. Keep it fun.

When individuals comply with what they are told to do, it doesn't mean they like it. When they start to find the fun in the activity, they are moving beyond compliance. This is the shift from doing something because they have to, to doing something because they want to. When observing changes in different groups, the biggest difference between the groups that were doing well and those that were only complying, was that those who were doing well were also enjoying it. They were enjoying the challenge of the change. They were actually finding ways to make it fun. They were smiling when they were trying the new things.

Those who were not having fun were acting as if they were being made to do it. They weren't smiling. If I were a mind reader, I am guessing I would have sensed someone in the non-smiling group thinking, "We're only doing this right now because you are making us. When you leave we'll go back to doing what we were doing before." Those who were having fun would probably say, "This is our thing now, not the boss's. We are going to have some fun, enjoy doing it and try different things to make sure this works for us." Why do something if it doesn't work? Why do something just for your boss and only because you have to? Why not have a little fun in the process?

Six Challenges to Making It Work

1.	I don't think this is working fast enough.
2.	Is this constant change or continuous improvement?
3.	Do we still have to observe, continue to reinforce and follow up?
4.	I don't think the reinforcement is working for us.
5.	I like the earlier success. Let's speed it up.
6.	There are just too many fires going on to take the time to focus on this change thing.

1. I don't think this is working fast enough.

You may find some evidence that what you are trying is not working. Resist the temptation to stop everything. It is probably not that bad. Address what is not working and find the small changes you can make that will ensure that efforts stay on track. Also examine areas where change is working well and identify the reasons it is working. Possibly you can apply the same strategies to areas where you are not seeing as much success. This exercise helps find ways to repeat good outcomes rather than stalling progress.

2. Is this constant change or continuous improvement?

One group of leaders I worked with said that the problem wasn't rapid change. They were good at that. For them, rapid change implied random, quick, constant change with no point. They experienced reorganizing, reengineering or restructuring about once a year, whether or not it was needed. That is not what is intended here. Continuous improvement is closer to the point rather than quick, knee-jerk changes that tug at you and pull you here and there almost randomly. Most people working in a large organization have experienced this kind of constant, directionless change.

3. Do we still have to observe, reinforce continued attempts and follow up?

The short answer is yes, if you want the changes to continue. When those who are accountable for the follow-up and pull-through are missing in action, this threatens the transition from compliance to commitment. Leaders must continue to observe and follow up to ensure not only that the changes are occurring but to ensure that individuals are giving the change an honest try.

Reinforcement from influencers is necessary if reinforcement is not yet in place from the employees, customers and the work. There may have been a lot of reinforcement for the kick-off and early attempts. Reinforcement should be given when employees modify the approach so that it works better and for the early signs of desired impact rather than just the attempts. Part of the challenge here is to also reinforce the influencers—the leaders, managers and supervisors. If you don't build that into your approach, you are often left with a good start but not much more. Reinforcement and continued active support from leaders (and for leaders) is necessary early and often throughout the *making it work phase.*

4. I don't think the reinforcement is working for us.

The appeal of reinforcing something can be strong. If you only reinforce activity without some connection to results, you may become frustrated that the reinforcement is not having the desired effect. If you only reinforce stories that sound good but that aren't true, then you may get more stories that aren't true. Be careful what you reinforce because you'll get more of it. Reinforce early and often attempts at desired outcomes. Be sure to check that these behaviors are being refined and move in the direction of the desired results.

When managers rely solely on reinforcement like pats on the back, saying "good job," being nice, using money to reinforce groups or throwing money at good outcomes, they are likely to fail. The reinforcement here may not be perceived as being genuine or effective. Shift the focus to consequences that matter as described earlier and to reinforcement that leads to self-reinforcement and questions that help performers reflect on the work.

5. I like the early success. Let's speed it up and add a few more things.

This is a common occurrence for any personal or professional change effort. At times, when there is excitement about the outcome or early successes, someone wants to turn up the heat. This may be fine and you may need to push through the change because you recognize you are on the right path, but if you take on so much that you can't possibly follow up and focus on the quality of what you are doing, you may end up crushing the effort.

6. There are just too many fires going on to take the time to focus on this change thing.

The most likely distractors to change are the unexpected issues and interruptions that interfere with your day. Making something work requires a proactive approach. Focusing on progressive change each day requires choice. Focusing on fires, issues, problems and exceptions will drive us back toward compliance. If you overreact, you are letting these conditions manage the change. A proactive approach helps anticipate and embrace the fires up front and to coach employees on how to prioritize so that they are proactive most of the time and address only the real fires that are inevitable in any organization.

Coaching When You Can't Be Face-to-Face —Sean's Story

Sean is the regional director in charge of sales for a team of about 100 salespeople. He manages 10 division managers. Sean had a problem. He needed to improve sales. He was holding his sales managers accountable for helping improve the sales numbers and the sales behaviors of the sales reps. The challenge was this—his managers only met face-to-face with their people about once a month. They had a formal process for these visits. The problem was how to keep behavior change going when they weren't there in-person. They talked a few times per week but those calls were about issues, problems or specific customer challenges.

How might the managers build in some small and frequent touch points on a more frequent basis that would keep the other behavior changes going when the sales manager was not present? How could he keep the momentum going rather than repeat the same conversation once a month?

To build a bridge between the field visits, Sean was interested in helping his sales managers develop proactive and helpful touch points to keep the behavior changes moving in the desired direction when they weren't there in person. To accomplish this, Sean was able to accelerate the rate of changes within his sales force.

Let's look at the scenario and what Sean was trying to accomplish.

When Sean and his team of managers were planning their approach to coaching, they had very specific result targets in mind. First on the list, but the one they would have to wait for, was sales results. The other measures were more near term. The indicators that would tell them they were on the right track were customer responses and rep responses to the coaching. The primary leading indicators were what they wanted customers to say and do on each call that would be signs of progress. They would plan on an anticipated response and then review what actually happened to evaluate progress.

To build in feedback from customers and reps, Sean and his team of sales managers did two things consistently. The sales managers had coaching touch points by phone with their sales reps and asked them what their plans were prior to each sales call. Pre-planning is not a new thing for this group but how they asked about the plans was very specific. They asked, "What do you want the customer to say or do during the sales call you are about to make?" The salespeople discussed the last sales call they made and described what the customer said or did. They built off of this to make sure they were moving the customer along a sales continuum. They specifically described what the customer had done and said on the last call prior to each subsequent call. They also described what they would say and do to elicit a desired response. Together they refined the initial call plan, not because the boss wanted them to, but because it would help elicit better customer responses.

The managers also encouraged the sales reps to identify a contingency plan that included other possible customer responses, other possible sales behaviors and other possible targets such as gatekeepers or other customers they encountered.

Soon after the call the manager and the sales rep discussed what happened. The rep began with what the customer said or did on the call. They then described what they did to prompt the customer responses.

Here's how it worked. Division managers reported helping more than they usually do when they are coaching. Their reps viewed these conversations as condensed coaching and focused on one to two behaviors over a sustained period of time. These conversations were mostly about moving the salesperson and the customer along the path of discretionary effort. The brevity forced both the seller and the coach to get to the point and to improve upon their focused behaviors.

Here's what Sean and the sales managers did to make it work. They took the initial tools and modified them in real time to work well for phone coaching conversations. They listened to their people and approached this as a project they were doing together. They asked a lot of questions to guide self-discovery. They asked questions about what they wanted customers to say and do. They followed up soon after the calls and asked questions first about customer responses before shifting to what the seller said or did. They also offered suggestions before and after calls to help create small changes in seller and customer behaviors. They asked the value question at the end of the coaching day to fine-tune their coaching and to ensure that they helped their direct reports. As stated earlier, the value question is essentially asking your direct reports how you helped them as a coach. This kind of feedback helps coaches improve their impact on a frequent basis (and the feedback can also be reinforcing). They created repetition within a day by having at least three calls like this over the course of a day and they did this a few times a month to pull the changes through.

What I Like about Sean's Story

This team took a very practical approach to change. They needed touch points to keep the changes going in between their face-to-face meetings.

- Sean and his team had a process and followed it. The process helped keep the coaches on track and was repeatable for each coach and sales rep.

- They built in several kinds of touch points that worked and helped. Some of these touch points mimicked the field visits. Some were built into their day-to-day conversations as brief, helpful, proactive touch points that were welcomed by their salespeople.

- The most startling thing about this approach is that influencers could see things working as the day progressed both within individuals and across individuals as the selling and the coaching were fine-tuned and improved upon.

Making it work emphasizes trying it, seeing it work and fine-tuning the approach. Continue to emphasize *deliberate impatience* and continue to talk about your line of sight. During this phase, begin to gather multiple examples that become part of the body of evidence. Refine the pinpoints and emphasize practice with repetition. Sean's story included ongoing ways to fine-tune the approach and finding ways to see it work.

This phase is where people typically give up. Just as in the *getting started phase*, the quicker you can pull the tips forward in the *making it work phase*, the quicker and better the sustainability will be. Repetition and continued refinement help. Setting reasonable expectations helps too. When you become more fluent at new behaviors and you see more and more of the desired results, you and your team are on your way to sustaining the change.

CHAPTER 8

GETTING IT TO STICK

The desired goal for most change efforts is to get the change to stick. How do you build in support to sustain the changes that are now observable? What additional changes are necessary to sustain the desired outcomes? How can you shift to helping individuals be self-managed so that the new behaviors will continue to be demonstrated, even when no one is looking?

During this phase, you may have achieved the desired results that were anticipated and planned months ago. If you look only at the end-point, you are in danger of soon losing the gains you have realized. If you look only to the outcomes and not the behaviors and habits that got to the end-point, you are unlikely to protect and sustain the changes.

Behavioral Science Helps

Getting it to stick still requires care, active involvement and deliberate application of the science of change. Here's how the science of change can help in this phase.

Five key elements of the science are reviewed here—
Fluency and Expertise, the S-Curve, Facilitating Change,
and Self-Reinforcement.

1. Fluency and Expertise

An understanding of fluency is worthwhile not only
when you are trying to get change to occur but also
when you want it to stick. Behavioral fluency includes
two dimensions—accuracy and speed. Focus first on
effectiveness before trying to do it fast. An individual
whose goal is attaining fluency at some skill attempts
many trials and gets real-time, immediate feedback on
accuracy. They are given the chance over many trials to
learn how to do something more accurately. Once they
master the content and can be accurate at it, a speed
dimension is added. For example, not only do they now
need to be accurate at answering questions, they must
answer the questions within a certain time period.

When you know something forwards and backwards,
you are able to access this information quickly. Fluency
drills help you to not only know something, but to
know it quickly. When you know something well, you
retain it longer and retrieve it quicker. In other words,
experts not only do things well, they often seem to perform in their area of expertise without effort or with
fluency—which is similar to what is commonly referred
to as *unconscious competence.*

When you only know something accurately now, but really need to think about it, you may struggle to remember it later. Think about the exams you crammed for when you were in school. When you pulled an all-nighter and crammed for that midterm, you might have done fine in the morning. But when it came time for the final, you needed to re-learn much of that information. When you studied over time and learned the information to the point that you didn't really need to think about it, you didn't need to spend that much time prior to the final getting ready for the test. You knew the material, so the studying was more of a refresher rather than re-learning information that you only knew at a superficial level.

2. The S-Curve

The S-Curve shows one way to depict how learning occurs. The graphic shows two approaches to learning. The straight line reflects the traditional approach to goal setting. The distance between goals is the same in the early, middle and later phases of development. The S-Curve on the other hand reflects how individuals typically learn. They start off slow and in need of reinforcement early and often. Everything is new and the new skill may be overwhelming.

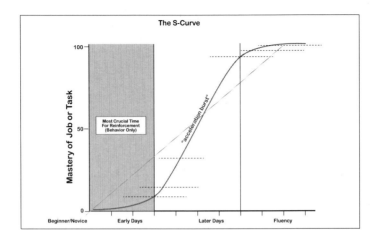

We all have experienced the beginning of the S-curve when we first learned to drive. There was a lot to know and do. We were nervous. We made mistakes and were afraid to make mistakes. The skill of driving may have been clear when we read about it, but then we had to do it. We improved slowly. Eventually with enough hours, repetition and practice, we began to pull it together and all of the learning components converged. This is when the change curve begins to accelerate. As novices we eventually reached the point when we were proficient drivers. The challenge later (and if you want to invest the additional effort) is to become an expert driver, which requires many more repetitions. The differences in what experts do are smaller differences but those differences have a big impact on the outcomes (if you are racing automobiles, for example). The changes at the top of the S-curve are small and take considerable time, repetition, appropriate feedback and reinforcement. It may take years and thousands of quality repetitions to become an expert. The key point here though is that the area after the acceleration point is where sustainability resides. It is the area where you could be on the verge of becoming an expert.

3. Facilitating Change

During the *getting it to stick phase,* facilitate change with those who know what to do and how to make it work. Help them find the small changes to help them reach fluency. Training and antecedents were the focus in the *getting started phase.* Coaching and questioning are the focus in the *making it work phase.* During this phase you are unlikely to help if you tell people what to do or ask only basic questions. Now figure out how to increase the self-management and accountability of the person who is learning. Become more deliberately collaborative when developing learning plans since sustainable plans are likely best arrived at through a discussion with the performers who are already pretty good at the skill being targeted. These individuals now need to decide (with your guidance) the best area to focus on that is likely to have the biggest impact.

4. Self-Reinforcement

Reinforcement from the work and the customer are still relevant in this phase. It is the transfer to self-reinforcement, creating a culture of continuous improvement and the emphasis on continued fine-tuning of behaviors that are important here. Enhancing self-reinforcement and observing your full impact are essential at this point. Individuals who have invested time in making it work are aware of what *good* looks like. Now is the time to help them see the real impact they are having on the outcomes.

Eight Suggestions for Getting Change to Stick

1.	Remember how you got here.
2.	Broaden areas of support.
3.	Build habit strength.
4.	Align compensation and other systems now.
5.	Introduce novelty.
6.	Manage the post-reinforcement pause.
7.	Encourage a culture of continuous improvement.
8.	Transfer, generalize and broaden impact.

1. Remember how you got here.

Behaviors matter. The process matters. When striving to achieve a result you may say you've arrived and then forget about or abandon the careful work, behaviors, skills and processes that got you there. Continue to manage both behaviors and results. You may not need to focus as much on reinforcing behaviors once you get to a certain level of performance, but still check in on how people are continuing to achieve high levels of performance. At this point, the behaviors are likely maintained by self-reinforcement and the reinforcement provided by the work, customers and coworkers. Reinforcement from the organization can help to maintain this level of performance but it is not the primary way to maintain it.

2. Broaden areas of support.

During the early phases, the messages about change may come from a few senior leaders. Over time, it will help to have other people also share these messages and demonstrate (through their behavior, their follow-up, reinforcement and the questions they ask) that they too are owners of the change and accountable for it over time. It also helps if more people are able to share examples of how they have experienced the change and influenced positive outcomes.

3. Build habit strength.

The concept of *habit strength* is important when trying to bring about sustainable changes. In the early phases you are either complying or just getting good at some of the new behaviors. When entering this phase, individuals may be engaging in desirable behaviors not because they have to or because they are trying new things to make them work, but because they automatically do things repeatedly that work. The challenge, of course, is to help initiate and sustain desirable habits that create the desired changes and the culture you are interested in sustaining.

4. Align compensation and other systems now.

Consider implementing changes in compensation and other systems during this phase. Many groups introduce system changes very early in a change process. Early is the wrong time for changing something as big and complex as the compensation system. First identify the behaviors and results you are interested in changing. Once the changes are put in place you can see where you need to add additional compensation and rewards, to both create and sustain the changes. When changes in compensation are introduced early, you aren't able to determine whether the changes in leader follow-up or the money created the improvement. Why throw money at something early when you may bring about those changes without additional compensation? Then compensation can be more deliberately and intentionally focused so that it will lead to a real return on your investment.

You may discover along the way that there are conflicts, inconsistencies or even clashes among different systems that are in place. During this phase, create alignment in these areas. If your organization has competing functions and silos, first improve the behaviors and change capabilities within the functions and silos. Finger-pointing across functions and silos is a common way to avoid change. Consider addressing this sooner only if the finger-pointing is becoming a constant obstacle and an excuse for delaying the functions and silos from taking their first steps.

5. Introduce novelty.

You've all gotten bored with something you've done repeatedly. Consider how to introduce novelty into work and activities to make them more fun, interesting and challenging. Novelty helps you break out of ruts and performance plateaus. Novelty helps keep your efforts fresh. Another take on novelty is evident in the leader who said that if he wasn't uncomfortable at least once every few weeks, he was in danger of not learning and not continuing to grow.

6. Manage the post-reinforcement pause.

When you have finally achieved something of importance, you may see a slight dip in effort. This dip in performance is called a *post-reinforcement pause*. It is predictable. Recognize that it is likely to happen and develop a plan for dealing with it. Anticipate it and allow it to happen for a brief period of time. Then encourage individuals to take deliberate actions to become re-engaged once they've had time to pause and look back on their accomplishments.

7. Encourage a culture of continuous improvement.

This concept should be introduced early in a change effort as part of ongoing communication. It may even be described as a *value* or a *desired culture*. Continuous improvement is a sustainability issue that you can introduce early and use as leverage to keep individuals and groups focused on persistently striving for excellence.

The point here is to always look to improve upon what is being done. This will be one of your only constants. The concept of continuous improvement helps to set these expectations early and provides an area of focus. It helps set high standards that encourage all to not just reach the top, but to continue to find ways to stay on top or even raise the bar.

It may be argued that someone can never become so good at certain behaviors that no room for improvement remains—especially those behaviors that have a positive impact on business results. Think about asking good questions. When do you get so good at these behaviors that you have nothing new to learn? You can spend your entire career enhancing the kinds of questions you ask and you'd still see the benefits in the answers you uncover or in the business results you achieve. The same is true for behaviors like active listening, effective planning, anticipating and overcoming objections or following up. These are behaviors that are likely to always have room for improvement and that room is filled with opportunity.

8. Transfer, generalize and broaden impact.

When something has had a good outcome and you can identify the behaviors that got you there, you can then determine how to transfer those behaviors to other areas and outcomes. Apply some of the same learning to other business results or even to other lines of business. One company had great success in an area of productivity and went on to use the same core process to attain better safety results.

What do you want to improve upon next? Consider the next layer you want to build upon the foundation created by the initial change.

Five Challenges to Getting Change to Stick

1.	Changing Direction
2.	Needing New Habits and Behaviors
3.	Recognizing When You've Hit a Plateau
4.	Forgetting Behaviors and Resting on Your Laurels
5.	Missing the Point

1. Changing Direction

You know a new change is just around the corner. Do your own assessment about whether you have built a foundation that will last or one that can be tweaked to fit the change in direction. The change in direction may be the next logical step in the progression. Consider using some of the core change skills that helped achieve the last change as you shift to a new direction. If you have selected behaviors that transfer and generalize, consider finding ways to build on the last change rather than shifting directions completely.

2. Needing New Habits and Behaviors

Sometimes conditions change and what got us here will not help us in the future. Evaluate your behaviors on an ongoing basis. The behaviors that helped us last year may be a good foundation for next year, but new behaviors and habits are needed to continue to grow, develop and improve the results. This may be the time to add new behaviors to help create new outcomes.

3. Recognizing When You've Hit a Plateau

You may see evidence of plateaus in behaviors or in results. When someone hits a plateau, first determine what kind of performance potential is being left on the table. If someone is close to the ceiling, you may not want to exert additional effort to close a small gap in performance. If you are stale or bored, you may need to find ways to introduce novelty into your approach. This is a good time to reach out to others to find examples from those who have not plateaued. Find out what they did to continue growing. Sometimes a results plateau has been reached because someone has stopped doing the things that got them to this level or they have taken a post-reinforcement pause since they have reached their goal. It may also be because they have not added new behaviors to help them reach the next level.

4. Forgetting Behaviors and Resting On Your Laurels

Eventually you run out of patience and return to the results. If you use your old approach of focusing on results without continuing to discuss and reinforce the right behaviors, you risk negatively impacting the results. There is some fragility to behavior change. If you neglect it and fail to care for it over time, a drop in results is likely.

Yes, changes can be fragile. The outcomes and results that you've achieved may be cause for celebration and may lead you to think you don't need to focus on change anymore. What better time to look for the next change than when you are on top of your game? What is the plan for staying on top? Have you ensured that your culture is one of continuous improvement where everyone is always looking for the next way to hone and enhance performance?

5. Missing the Point

You can miss the point in several ways when attempting to achieve change quickly and sustainably. One way is to get obsessed with squeezing out the small changes that make only small differences. If closing a performance gap takes you off track, skip it. It may not be worth it. And there are plenty of other behaviors that are in need of significant improvement.

It's tempting to get enamored with the new activity, process or behavior and continue to do it even if it doesn't work, help or lead to the desired outcomes. It is like a pendulum that swings from results only to activity only. Balance is needed in any change. If the behavior change is not having the desired effect and you have tried to make it work, then perhaps you've selected the wrong behavior, process or activity. This was true in many of the quality programs in the last few decades. Winners of special awards were listed as among the highest quality organizations around and then some of them went out of business soon afterward. The activities and quality auditing became the focus rather than balanced results. Quality standards like ISO 9000 were written to assess compliance with standards, not the success of the business entity. Compliance with ISO 9000 was used by some companies for marketing purposes rather than to improve business health.

Going It Alone—Brett's Story

Brett is a leader within a large manufacturing organization. If you are in a different industry, please keep reading. Brett can help you. He found some ways to streamline his approach to rapid change. He was attempting to influence several thousand employees through four different regions and eight senior leaders across each of those four regions. Brett's team had been through several other change initiatives in the past. They had put a quality program in place. They were now attempting to transition to a High Performance Work System across all of these employees and across all of their geographic regions. After Brett and his team were handed the details of the implementation, they knew it was too big as it was currently defined. They could have felt overwhelmed and they could have panicked. The organization has high expectations for Brett and his team. They pay close attention to key measures such as productivity, quality, compliance and safety.

Brett and his team were open to some of the methods of rapid change. They agreed to apply some of the tools in their workplace. They also agreed to use a rapid change process to improve one well-defined problem they were facing. Together they worked to develop some targets for their change. They attempted to break down the problems they faced into component behaviors. Initially they struggled to come up with something that would work for Brett's team of leaders. He could have told them to just comply in order to complete the training exercise, but instead he made an initial intervention that helped to redirect the process to an important business issue. The group decided to apply the rapid change process, which is described in detail in the next section, to the operation of one machine within each of the facilities—and this was not a small machine. They then broke down into component parts the behaviors that were necessary to operate the machines quickly and well.

There was a significant opportunity for improvement within the process of how workers transitioned between shifts. Individuals who work on one machine throughout a shift are encouraged to keep the machine going at all costs even if shutting down a machine to repair it may be better over the long term. Brett had an additional challenge. He was held accountable for keeping the change going but was given few additional resources to help him bring about the change.

He made a few additions to the processes that were essential to its success. He decided to check in with teams of his direct reports—groups of two senior leaders per region—for about 15 minutes per week for a four-week period. That's an hour of his time within a week. Can you devote an hour of your time if that hour makes a big difference? During the brief touch point check-ins he asked his team members to share their best examples of how they were using the rapid change process within each of their areas of accountability. He did not have a long agenda. He did not even have the answers. He asked simple questions and asked direct reports to describe what they were seeing and hearing in their areas.

Brett started to notice a few things. His team members were attempting to try new things on a weekly basis. Team members were doing something each day and week. Operators were pushing for details to make sure the process worked for them.

Brett's team members identified a way to influence all of their managers and supervisors and to give them some tools and tips that had a high probability of working. During the initial training, the importance of The 3-Minute Meeting™ was stressed. The team members decided they needed a short list of questions that everyone would try daily. They wanted to make it easy and convenient for others to ask these questions so they turned the questions into a tool, by typing them up and laminating them. Here is the list that this team came up with to help them apply some of the rapid change technology to their workplace.

Questions: The 3-Minute Meeting™
What worked well today?
Why do you think that worked?
What is your best example this week that illustrates what is working well?
What did you learn that you didn't know?
How have I helped you?
What did you do specifically that worked well today?
How did you modify your approach to make it work better?
How are you helping team members this week?
How are you or the team getting better?
How did you do that? (Ask this after you observe something you like.)

Brett and his team also got on the phone every three to four weeks over a three-month period to share examples of their successes. They shared good examples using a fairly systematic approach. In the beginning, they discovered that the process worked in their area. They were able to share examples of how rapid change led to improvements in shift handoffs and that it also led to measurable improvements in the performance of their machines. They kept at it and continued to fine-tune their process. Brett continued to check in for 15 minutes every week or so. Brett's team continued to talk about it as a group every four weeks. Then a few other things happened. The frontline employees, through the questions that were asked repeatedly by the supervisors, managers and directors started to take ownership for their areas of responsibility. They started to own their work areas. Employees started to come up with ideas to make other small changes. As long as the changes were not catastrophic, they were given permission to make those changes even when management thought it wouldn't work. More and more small changes were put in place. More and more input from employees started to emerge. The successes were also extended by the employees to areas beyond the initial productivity focus. Employees started to apply their questions to safety and quality without prompting and without being required to do so.

What I Like about Brett's Story

Let's review this example to identify the elements that helped to bring about the change.

1. The senior manager held frequent but brief weekly follow-up sessions—touch points. They were able to see the initial plan start to work sooner rather than later.

2. Managers saw their questions work so they kept asking them.

3. The group viewed fine-tuning as an essential skill.

4. The group met or spoke monthly via conference call to share good examples and the details about what worked.

5. The group accepted and acted upon feedback from Brett, direct reports and others.

6. The group shifted the initial focus on the behaviors of the frontline employees and shifted their impact to other managers and leaders to raise their level of influence.

7. They generalized the technique and approach to other business issues beyond machine shift changes. The group started to apply these methods to safety and other business challenges.

Success is earned through ongoing ways of making it work. Brett and his team held each other accountable and found ways to see it work over time. They used The 3-Minute Meeting™ to guide this change and to create new habits. They were able to point to a body of evidence since not only did they see the behaviors work, they were able to see the results improve.

The path has progressed from getting started, to the daily challenges of making it work, to fluency and sustainability. The science of change can help accelerate your progress and can help achieve more of the long-term goals you desire. In the next few chapters the specific tactics of these Coaching for Rapid Change sessions will be reviewed. This includes a review of what a rapid change session is and how to facilitate and troubleshoot the sessions when things go off-track. A tool will also be reviewed to plan, organize and implement large-scale change from the first 30 days through 24 months using the working backward process. The key here is to have a process, work it and improve it over time. The process will connect behaviors today to results later.

SECTION III

APPLICATION TOOLS AND TIPS

This section includes several tools and tips that can be used by individuals, teams and organizations. The tools can be used to help leaders and managers to influence change along the path to optimal performance. Coaching for Rapid Change® includes the tactics of how influencers are guiding others along this path. Included are details on how to facilitate Coaching for Rapid Change sessions and how to troubleshoot challenges along this path. One additional tool is the 30-60-90-day plan and 12-month vision which helps leaders and organizations connect behaviors to long-term outcomes, starting now and building toward some future state. This tool serves as a behavioral vision that is focused, intentional and in the present. This ultimately helps you move in the right direction to achieve the desired results.

CHAPTER 9

COACHING FOR RAPID CHANGE A STARTER KIT

This chapter offers a "how to" for those interested in actually influencing and coaching incrementally toward optimal performance. To accelerate the rate of change, brief helpful touch points are necessary. The touch points include the following:

- Setting expectations the first time you address something with an employee

- Following up over the course of days and weeks as the coach asks employees how it is working, how the customer is responding and how they are improving

- Tweaking and fine-tuning along the way

- Listening to those you are trying to help and asking them good questions

- Building in some self-assessment and self-reinforcement

- Directly observing and asking questions about what happened

Taken together, these are the essentials of any good coaching approach.

Accelerate the rate of change here by increasing the quality and frequency of the touch points. Coaching for Rapid Change sessions, outlined later, are the mechanism for talking about fine-tuning your touch points and finding how to build in different kinds of coaching touch points that work for both the employee and the coach. The sessions provide a forum for talking specifically about what worked and identifying the small changes that will accelerate the change or improve its sustainability. These sessions provide a forum for learning from others who are trying to influence change in similar situations. It helps improve how to do this better in real time.

This section is about how to use the sessions to help bring about rapid change within your team, work group or organization. The phases discussed in the previous section can be used to guide your application during the sessions. First, follow the process as it is described here. Start it today with a group of individuals who are influencing others who want to accelerate the rate of change. Then, over the course of weeks, modify the approach described here to make it work for you and your organization. You will discover enhancements and improvements along the way. After a few months, if you have successfully made some small changes to your process, have done so with enough repetition and have seen the value in it, you will likely enter the *getting it to stick phase*.

Improving the Quality of Touch Points

The method for Coaching for Rapid Change® is a technique for taking a step back from the day-to-day activities and touch points that are driving the change. It is a way to tweak the approach to change in a systematic and repetitive way. Getting supervisors, managers or leaders together to take a step back every few weeks or so will help you not only find out how you are bringing about change, but it will also help you accelerate the rate of change. If short, but frequent touch points define the hours and days as you attempt to manage change, Coaching for Rapid Change® sessions offer a way to continue what is working well and fine-tuning what is not at a weekly or biweekly level.

An underlying assumption rooted in the technology of change is that there is significant value in identifying what is working and more importantly what coaches are specifically doing that is working. Individuals are paid for doing something, not avoiding something. Yet when looking at manager and leader behaviors in organizations, you often see an overemphasis on managing exceptions, problems and challenges. These are areas worth investigating on occasion but an overemphasis on exceptions and problems will create mere compliance and suboptimal performance. If you only focus on what is broken, the kind of culture instilled will be one of negative reinforcement and punishment. Individuals then will work to meet the minimum requirements and will work hard to fly below the radar. Individuals will be reluctant to share bad news. This can also lead to stagnation and complacency. I've heard it described as keeping their heads above water and staying below the radar.

Getting Started with Coaching for Rapid Change Sessions

Coaching for Rapid Change® is a structured session for helping those who influence change to talk about what is working and how they can enhance what they are doing with some degree of frequency and repetition. It requires individuals to come prepared with good examples of how they are influencing change. These sessions ideally include individuals who coach and influence change. They could include an executive and his or her managers. They could include a manager and his or her supervisors.

Consider this—If individuals are accountable for having impact and their job is to influence change, why not set a standard that they have at least one good example each week of bringing about impactful change through positive means? Everyone has an occasional bad day, but if a person strings together five bad days in a row, then you aren't getting your money's worth for that person's time. Coaching for Rapid Change sessions allow senior leaders to observe and hear about how supervisors, managers and leaders are bringing about positive change in their areas of influence.

A Coaching for Rapid Change® Session

Here's what a Coaching for Rapid Change session looks like. A group of managers gets together with their manager to discuss how they have influenced change in the last few weeks. These sessions work best with 6 to 10 managers per session. Each manager shares a specific example of how he or she has influenced change in that time period. The example can be about a specific individual or a specific team. Each manager shares a concrete example that includes the outcomes, the behaviors of the employee(s) and the coaching/influence behaviors that helped to bring about the changes. As each example is being shared, it is being facilitated and timed by the leader of this group. All others are taking notes as each example is being shared. At the end of each example, the facilitator encourages others to share feedback of a specific kind. This includes what they liked, since this is about repeating what actually works in the near term. It also includes suggestions and questions that prompt additional positive feedback or additional refinement. This will be expanded upon later in the chapter, but this is the overall structure. A reasonable time period is 30 to 60 minutes for these kinds of meetings. Any longer than that and the session becomes tedious and punishing. Before reviewing this structure in detail, let's first discuss feedback a bit more.

Feedback, Coaching and Reinforcement

Feedback and coaching are two areas that overlap. In its simplest form, feedback is information. It is tactical, objective and used for evaluation. Coaching is relationship-based. It can be subjective and is often developmental. Good coaching includes various kinds of feedback to the individual regarding his or her previous performance and impact. That information is used to develop a path forward based on what did and did not work in the past.

The best kinds of feedback involve self-discovery and assessment. Effective feedback requires trust among individuals, and to do it well, a high degree of emotional intelligence.

According to the science, reinforcement simply increases the future likelihood of behavior. In this sense, feedback that is "positive" and feedback that is "constructive" can have the effect of being positive reinforcement for individuals if it is delivered in the right way. The Coaching for Rapid Change® session is intended to create conditions where both positive and constructive bits of feedback can potentially positively reinforce the future occurrence of valuable behavior and create conditions of continuous improvement along the path of discretionary effort. Conversely, not all feedback is reinforcing. In practice, it may serve to stop or diminish behavior. The Coaching for Rapid

Change® session is intended to increase the chance that any feedback, whether positive or constructive, is reinforcing to the person who receives it.

The Tactics of a Coaching for Rapid Change Session

> ### Tips
> 1. Listen and take notes
> 2. Speak in bullets
> 3. Be precise, concise and specific
>
> #### How to Share Good Examples (total time: 5 minutes)
> Ask:
> 1. What are you trying to accomplish? Briefly describe the business result, 1-2 desired customer responses and 1-2 employee behaviors. **(1 min.)**
> 2. How is it working? (2 min.)
> 3. What are you—as a coach—specifically doing to help? (2 min.)
>
> #### How to Provide Feedback (total time: 5 minutes)
> + Describe what you liked (no need to repeat what has already been said)
> ? Ask clarifying questions
> Δ Provide 1-2 suggestions to help
>
> © 2010 Aubrey Daniels International
>
> **Rapid Change Sessions**

The facilitator begins each Coaching for Rapid Change® session by reviewing the process and outcomes for the session. Participants in the session are encouraged to listen to what is shared in the session and to take good notes. This will help ensure that the feedback they are to provide later is objective and based on what individuals say or do. That is, it helps listeners focus on behavior. Participants are encouraged to speak in bullets and to be precise, concise and specific. The facilitator reminds participants that sharing of good examples and the feedback after each example will be timed.

How to Share Good Examples

Volunteers will each share a good coaching example in the format outlined here.

1. Coaches will describe what they are trying to accomplish. Specifically, they will describe the one result or outcome they are currently focusing on. They will also describe which one or two short-term results (leading indicators) they are attempting to change now that will help them achieve the long-term results and outcomes they desire. In customer-facing jobs, this includes desirable customer responses that are leading indicators that change is occurring. Coaches then identify the one or two employee behaviors that are likely to have a positive impact on the desired leading indicators and results.

   This initial segment should take one minute or less. A few cautions here. When a coach is too expansive in this section, it is often evidence that the coaching is unclear or the coaching area is too big for the employee or the coach to see observable changes any time soon. When the coach spends most of the time talking about what he or she is going to do, it may also be a sign that they aren't doing anything or aren't following up properly with the person they are attempting to influence. It may be that they've had an initial conversation but not much more than that. To go beyond just getting change to occur once, demonstrate consistent evidence of pull-through and follow-up.

2. Coaches then describe what is actually happening. This is at the heart of rapid change and essential to identifying the kinds of improvements that are possible and the coaching behaviors that influence change. The coach specifically describes how the current brief plan is working. This segment includes trends in performance, changes in employee behavior, leading indicators and any initial impact on the business result or outcome. Discussing how the plan is working helps managers describe not only moments of change that they have seen on a specific day, but also how the change has been observed over the course of weeks and months. It is important that this part of the discussion be about some recent change. This segment should take about two minutes and includes the specific, observable impact of the coach's work.

3. Lastly, coaches then describe specifically what they have done to ensure that the coaching is working and helping. Coaches describe here what they did to bring about the change. They describe the proactive behaviors they used.

They describe any in-the-moment changes they have made. They describe the words they used to get change started or any questions they asked to ensure that they got others involved in the change process.

Each example is put through a rapid change process to learn how it happened but to also help replicate the outcomes with similar situations others are likely to face. The details are important to achieve specific outcomes and to accelerate the rate of change. It ensures that the successful change behaviors are clearly described. This includes clear descriptions of impact on results, leading indicators and employee behaviors. It ensures clear descriptions of what managers and leaders have done that are both proactive and deliberate. This helps other managers replicate manager behaviors that have been proven to work. The session ensures that touch points prompt, guide and accelerate change. This builds in consistency and a structure that guides change over time rather than building in events that are disconnected.

Guiding Real-Time Feedback

After each example is shared, encourage immediate, active and objective feedback. This feedback is weighted heavily in favor of focusing on what you liked and what worked, not for any soft reason, but because it is likely to be reinforcing to the employee and the behavior of the coach. It also helps others know how to replicate good results through specific behaviors.

As each good example is shared, encourage everyone to take notes as they listen to the examples of what others are doing. Sharing feedback by using notes increases the quality of objective feedback.

At the end of each example, encourage the other participants to quickly share feedback to the person who offered the example using the following specific format:

1. What did you like? Or what should the person keep doing? Or what will you borrow?

This is the first bit of feedback shared. It is not meant to be nice, soft, positive or upbeat, though it can be. The point here is to increase the chances that good things are repeated and to identify the likely drivers of change. It also helps the group share the specific tactics that have created the changes. Do this by focusing on the behaviors you want more of in the future.

2. Ask clarifying questions to better understand the example.

Do this next because sometimes the examples are too short and critical information is left out. Do this after "what we liked" because the habits in many change situations are to grill people and to find fault. The questioning here is to clarify what and how things worked.

It is also helpful to ask these questions before suggestions are shared, since some suggestions may come across as criticism.

3. Provide one or two suggestions (total) for each example to help the person improve what they are trying to accomplish.

Limit the number of suggestions here. The suggestions are designed to help make small changes to enhance what someone is doing, not to overwhelm them with 50 things or to just tell them what they did wrong. The burden here is on the individuals providing feedback. Find the one or two best suggestions that are likely to help this coach the most over the next few weeks. This requires very pointed, objective and actionable feedback.

Timing

These sessions last about 30 to 60 minutes. A 30-minute meeting duration is an easier way to start this process. In a 30-minute session, up to three examples can be shared. A 60-minute meeting can include up to six good examples. There is plenty of flexibility here and other options are viable. A meeting of 60-minutes is used here as a starting point to illustrate a sample meeting format.

An example is shared. Take five minutes for each example including the following:

- What are you trying to accomplish? (This takes

about one minute.)

- How is it working? (This takes about two minutes.)
- What are you doing specifically to help? (This takes about two minutes.)

Feedback from others is provided (up to five minutes per example).

- Share feedback right after each example.
- Emphasize what you liked.
- Try to limit suggestions to just one or two.
- Move on after five minutes. If people who provide feedback have more to share, if it is important they can do so after the meeting.

A Sample Agenda

An agenda for getting started with this process looks something like this.

Coaching for Rapid Change Session: Sample Agenda for 60-Minute Meeting	
Opening by Leader/Facilitator	(10 minutes)
Good Example #1	(5 minutes)
Feedback on Example #1	(5 minutes)
Good Example #2	(5 minutes)
Feedback on Example #2	(5 minutes)
Good Example #3	(5 minutes)
Feedback on Example #3	(5 minutes)
Good Example #4	(5 minutes)
Feedback on Example #4	(5 minutes)
Review of Commitments for Next Meeting	(10 minutes)
Total time:	**60 minutes**

Why Take this Kind of Approach?

The tactics described here provide a mechanism for harnessing our impatience with the speed of change. When listening to a Coaching for Rapid Change® session, all participants are able to see and hear details that provide early evidence that change is happening. Hold each other accountable for having brief, objective change plans. Hold each other accountable for not just having a plan, but also for the impact of the plan. Because it also includes "the how" of the change—what the influencers did to accelerate the rate of change—emphasize not just outcomes and results that are likely to occur over time—as lagging indicators—but behaviors that can occur now.

The pressures to change are around you on a daily basis. Organizations that are able to manage change well and bring about deliberate, observable change within their own workforce are at a distinct advantage. Coaching for Rapid Change® sessions help groups not only survive the changes that are all around them, but also attack change deliberately and proactively. The techniques and methods described above can help you achieve change quickly on your own and in a way that creates many of the outcomes you have heard about in the stories and examples that appear throughout this book.

Replicate before you deviate. When you are getting started with this process, replicate the structure and process for the first two or three times. Then consider what small changes you can make to the session to make it work better for you and your team. This chapter provides the nuts and bolts of a Coaching for Rapid Change® session. It includes the tactics and the fundamental tools to achieve change through a persistent and proactive approach.

The next chapter contains tips to help you facilitate and troubleshoot the process. It also provides additional details on how to fine-tune your sessions to make them work better within your workplace.

CHAPTER 10

FINE-TUNING YOUR SESSIONS

This chapter includes additional details on fine-tuning the Coaching for Rapid Change® session and in navigating the *making it work phase* effectively. It is about moving beyond complying with the process to finding ways to make the sessions work over time. This chapter includes details on how to facilitate the sessions, how to refine them, and how to troubleshoot inevitable blips, obstacles and any resistance that you may encounter along the way.

Facilitating a Coaching for Rapid Change® Session

Set-Up

Designate a facilitator for each session. These sessions require that the facilitator remains on track to ensure that good habits are developed right from the start.

Sessions should be set up in advance with a clear understanding of what you are trying to change. Be specific about the requirements. One hour per session is about right, although I've seen some great 30-minute meetings. This is really up to you based on the kind of work you do and the culture within your organization.

Sessions should be timed. Ask that examples be shared in five minutes or less per person. This can vary of course. The important part here is to set the expectation that the examples are timed. This helps to set up self-correction. Individuals may rush through examples initially so this may require prompting them to add a little more detail, usually in the areas of what happened or what they did to help. Encourage participants to speak in bullets and to be precise, concise and specific when they share examples and when they provide feedback.

Sessions can be conducted in person or by conference call. If you can do these sessions in person initially, it will likely help you get on track sooner. Use the phone options if individuals are located in different physical locations, but if possible, set the meetings up in person at least for the first three or four sessions.

During the Session

Ask for a volunteer to go first and ask that person to explain the situation that they are trying to improve and with whom. Be sure to tell the person to wrap up the coaching example around the five-minute mark. The goal here is to share good examples and not performance problems.

Listen to the answers. Be patient and let people be uncomfortable in the beginning as you shape the sessions.

They may be uncomfortable with moments of silence. Use the silence to encourage them to share feedback. They may be uncomfortable speaking in bullets. It may take a few sessions to ensure most people become precise, concise and specific.

Take notes so you can go back and ask questions. Encourage others to take notes by reinforcing individuals who are taking notes. You can simply remind others to take notes since it will make the feedback more objective. You can also ask people to review their notes and share one thing they wrote down that they liked about the shared example.

Use facilitation questions to guide the learning. When facilitating a Coaching for Rapid Change® session, ask questions to help the person sharing the example provide good details. Here are a few examples:

- "What are you seeing him/her say or do?"
- "What specifically did the customer say?"
- "Tell us a little more about how it's working."
- "What else did you do to help?"
- "What worked?"
- "What is your next step?"

Ensure the group is providing feedback after each example. Starting with what you liked is essential to this process. It builds on specific actions that should be repeated or replicated by others. The point of the feedback is to enhance influencing skills. As the facilitator, hold your feedback to allow others a chance to share first. If no one shares critical feedback that you have identified, share it after others have offered their feedback and use your feedback as a way to transition to the next step in the process. Share what you liked and then transition to asking others what clarifying questions they have.

Encourage each person who offers examples or feedback. A good session includes having many participants offer small bits of information. At the end of the session, thank everyone for their participation. Recap what everyone should be doing and what went well.

When you are doing your first couple of sessions, ask individuals to provide feedback on the one or two things they will be doing based on the session. Individuals may struggle with this in the *getting started phase.* This closing question works very well in the *making it work phase.* If individuals are not able to identify how they are going to improve their coaching as a result of this session, then it is likely that the session is not adding optimal value to the participants. These sessions should work. "Working" is learning something during the session that you didn't know prior to the session. You may simply ask what others have written down or the one thing they learned that they didn't know at the beginning of the session.

Once the group becomes good at the sessions, you can change facilitators. When multiple team members can facilitate these sessions, they help keep sessions on track, since they know the ground rules and guidelines. They also help to keep the process going when the primary facilitator is not available. This is also a way to spread accountability for owning the change across more team members.

Troubleshooting Your Sessions

When starting the sessions, first attempt to do the process as you understand it. This is similar to the "try it" recommendation in the earlier chapter. Try this process. Then try to make it work. When I've seen individuals implementing these kinds of processes, some common issues come up.

Most of the suggestions here can be used when implementing any new process. We'll use an "If/Then" approach here as a way to describe the situation and offer a suggestion to solve it.

The session feels punishing.

If the sessions are beginning to feel punishing, two common causes are likely. You could be slipping back into focusing on managing exceptions, which leads individuals to do something only to avoid getting in trouble. Or, you may be forcing the process as compliance, without then shifting to making it work. This ultimately results in a lack of value in the sessions.

Then find ways to infuse more positive reinforcement into the meetings. The sessions should be fun but this doesn't mean it has to be canned or lacking in business focus. Ask the group to discuss this openly and to describe a way to make the sessions more helpful, valuable and fun. It may also help to ask about how the sessions are working and helping as a way to build in more value.

You aren't learning anything new.

If it doesn't seem like anything new is being offered, it is likely due to a lack of specificity in the examples being shared. If someone says that when they coached, they asked a bunch of good questions and provided some reinforcement, it may seem that they already know that these are important things to do in general. However, such statements don't tell you what to do *specifically*. What questions worked? How specifically did you attempt to reinforce? The answers to these questions will lead to new learning.

Then ask a few follow-up questions to help individuals share the details that describe what actually brought about the changes.

Participants ramble.

If participants are rambling and going on and on, it is likely due to how the sessions have been facilitated.

Then reset the requirements for the meeting at the start of the next meeting. Remind individuals about the need to time each segment. Remind them of the necessity for speaking in bullets and being precise, concise and specific. These are the antecedents, of course, and these alone won't do much to change this long term. The real change element will be following up immediately by reinforcing what is desirable—clear, concise discussion—and correcting in the moment when people exceed the time limit. Tell someone the time is up and ask them to stop. Interrupting may be necessary to reset the group's expectations about these meetings. It may also help to rotate facilitators as you are resetting the process. When you let someone ramble and you don't interrupt, everyone suffers. When you correct someone in the moment, you may rub the person who was interrupted the wrong way, but you are also ensuring that others don't have to hear all of the rambling.

The Session Turns into One of Our Usual Meetings.

If the Coaching for Rapid Change® session somehow morphed into your typical meetings, it may be due to facilitation or to scheduling your sessions back to back or as part of your regular meeting.

Then separate your Coaching for Rapid Change® sessions (in time) from your regular meetings. Reset the facilitation and meeting agenda requirements as described above.

Individuals are Not Coming to the Sessions Prepared.

If individuals are not coming to the sessions with good examples, it is likely due to a perception that this too shall pass, or that no one will call them on it, or perhaps due to a perception that there is no value in this kind of approach.

Then reset the expectations on why this is being done. One point worth noting is that new things won't work if you don't try them at least once. A few honest attempts at something new are required to have any chance at seeing it work. This challenge often requires following up after the session to encourage more people to try to get more good examples. It may also require simple things like leaders asking individuals to share brief, good examples throughout the week. When you are able to gather enough good examples, the facilitator can then ask people to share things that they heard were working and build on those kinds of successes.

Sustaining this process requires enough good repetition and seeing evidence that the sessions work over time. It requires building a habit in the process at the organizational level where individuals know how to work the process—facilitators and coaches—and where leaders support the frequency of the sessions over time. This requires progressive steps and markers that include results as well as a variety of behaviors.

The sessions help uncover what is hiding in plain sight. They also help unlock the good examples, ideas, behaviors and experiences of the people who are attempting the change on a daily and weekly basis. The sessions can help you demonstrate your appreciation and respect for the hard work of others. They also help peers learn from each other with some consistency. Now the challenge is how to organize this work over a significant period of time. The next chapter includes a roadmap for how to get change started in the first 30 days, how to make it work over the next 60 and 90 days, and how to strive for sustainability over the next 12 months.

CHAPTER 11

A BEHAVIORAL VISION 30 DAYS TO 12 MONTHS

This chapter describes an additional tool to help create incremental changes across time. The incremental changes include what behaviors and results will look like in the *getting started, making it work,* and *getting it to stick phases.* This tool helps you identify priorities and potential areas of focus and helps specify what good behaviors look like as you wait for the results. It shapes what you should be impatient about and when you should be patient. It also serves as a behavioral vision that maps out the details of the path forward. It is the implementation plan for now and for later. There is no magic in the time periods, which could be 30, 60, 90, or 360 days. The panels of 30, 60, or 90 days should include an immediate-state panel and another panel that is one or two years out. The gradients in the in-between panels really vary by the kind of change you are attempting to arrange. This is also a tool that leaders and others who sponsor change can use to commit to, not just for others, but also for themselves as they plan and coordinate large-scale changes.

Linking Changes Today to Long-Term Results Later

The Working Backward Model (introduced in Chapter 3) helps link behaviors now and later to related results over periods of time. A blank version of a tool is often introduced during a sponsor session, which is the initial meeting where leaders link the long-term changes to behaviors today and create the behavioral vision for the change effort. This model is meant to anchor any behavior change to a long-term business outcome. It also includes a long-term vision of what people will be saying and doing that is evidence of the targeted change. Four samples of a completed plan are included on the following pages to represent progression over time.

CRITICAL BEHAVIORS AND RESULTS					
Leader Behavior	Manager Behavior	Supervisor Behavior	Employee Behavior	Customer Responses	Results

CRITICAL BEHAVIORS AND RESULTS

30 DAY PLAN

Leader Behavior	Manager Behavior	Supervisor Behavior	Employee Behavior	Customer Responses	Results
• Coaches managers by asking for good examples	• Coaches supervisors by asking for good examples	• Observes and takes notes to capture objective feedback for team sessions and customer interactions	• Participates in a facilitated team-selling session	• Asks us a lot more questions	Deepen customer relationships
• Observes Rapid Change sessions and offers reinforcement	• Observes rapid change sessions and offers reinforcement	• Offers feedback and recognition. Does not always see positive benefits of this feedback.	• Begins to ask questions about the customer	Sample customer responses	• Examples or anecdotes of specific teams that have used the team-selling planning sessions to deepen customer relationships
• Begins to ask more questions rather than relying on telling	• Begins to ask more questions rather than relying on telling	• Begins to ask more questions about customers and the value they provide. These questions have the desired impact only some of the time.	• Learns more about customers and the capabilities of peers	• "I didn't know you offered that."	• Increase in frequency of joint calls and the number of people involved in joint call planning
• Begins to communicate the goals of a customer-centered results through desirable behaviors. Sometimes sends mixed messages.	• Begins to communicate the goals of customer-centered results through desired behaviors. Sometimes sends mixed messages.	• Avoids taking over customer calls and helps direct reports before or after these calls	• Begins to experience small wins during team-selling planning sessions	• "You really know my business."	• Increase in the number of client meetings scheduled and held
• Makes attempts to reinforce employees when they share challenges and tell the truth. Sometimes reinforces undesired behavior. Sometimes punishes desirable behavior.	• Makes attempts to reinforce employees when they share challenges and tell the truth. Sometimes reinforces undesired behavior. Sometimes punishes desirable behavior.	• Asks team members to identify roadblocks and offers solutions	• Initially talks about only a few customers in an attempt to have impact and because they are not fluent in desired behaviors	• "I didn't even think about that."	
• Shares messages about the value of acknowledging and encouraging continuous incremental improvement in performance.	• Shares messages about the value of acknowledging and encouraging continuous, incremental improvement in performance.	• Reinforces attempts and compliance with team-selling behaviors and process		• "Let's meet again."	
• Attempts to gather feedback on the value of their coaching	• Attempts to gather feedback on the value of their coaching				

175

CRITICAL BEHAVIORS AND RESULTS

60 DAY PLAN

Leader Behavior	Manager Behavior	Supervisor Behavior	Employee Behavior	Customer Responses	Results
• Coaches managers by asking for good examples	• Coaches supervisors by asking for good examples	• Provides helpful, objective feedback for team multiple examples of selling sessions and customer interactions based on observations and notes	• Beginning to experience multiple examples of bringing value to customers through working collaboratively with others	Sample customer responses (in addition to the previous list):	• Deepen customer relationships
• Observes rapid change sessions and offers reinforcement	• Observes rapid change sessions and offers reinforcement			• "That was easier than I thought."	• Customer satisfaction score
• Asks questions when coaching and when assessing their impact as coaches	• Asks questions when coaching and when assessing their impact as coaches	• Offers feedback and recognition. Begins to see positive impact of this feedback.	• Discusses and explores potential customer needs before discussing products	• "I want to introduce you to my friends."	• Customer retention
• Encourages customer-centered results through desirable behaviors that are in alignment with team selling. Sometimes sends mixed signals about balance between results and behaviors.	• Encourages customer centered results through desirable behaviors that are in alignment with team selling. Sometimes sends mixed signals about balance between results and behaviors.	• Asks more of the right questions about customers and the value they provide. These questions have the desired impact more and more often.	• Asks value questions after every customer and team interaction and is beginning to find useful information that can accelerate the team impact	• "I want to bring my partner to the meeting."	Revenue
				• "I think I brought the right information to this meeting. What additional information do you need?"	• Product per household
• Reinforces employees when they share challenges and tell the truth. Assesses impact of their leadership on others.	• Reinforces employees when they share challenges and tell the truth. Assesses impact of their leadership on others.	• Coaches direct reports and teams before and after customer interactions to prepare them for effective meetings	• Learns best practices from others and applies those practices to ongoing team selling planning sessions	• "What can I expect from this relationship?"	• Per new customer
• Begins to see the value of acknowledging and encouraging continuous incremental improvement in performance	• Begins to see the value of acknowledging and encouraging continuous, incremental improvement in performance	• Helps remove roadblocks and offers solutions that work	• Asks questions that have a high probability of gathering useful information	• "I really appreciate you bringing other sales specialists together on my behalf."	Employee retention and engagement
					• Increase in referrals
• Gathers ongoing feedback on the value of their coaching	• Gathers ongoing feedback on the value of their coaching	• Addresses compliance with team-selling behaviors and process initially by focusing on value to customer and on how the process works			• Increase in number of meetings, number of people per meeting
					• Increase in requests and questions from customers

176

CRITICAL BEHAVIORS AND RESULTS

90 DAY PLAN

Leader Behavior	Manager Behavior	Supervisor Behavior	Employee Behavior	Customer Responses	Results
• Coaches managers by providing quick and frequent feedback on what they liked and offers suggestions for incremental improvement	• Coaches supervisors by providing quick and frequent feedback on what they liked and offers suggestions for incremental improvement	• Asks questions on customer impact and the value of their coaching	• Takes responsibility for bringing value to customers through working collaboratively with others	• Calls you for advice • Involves you early in the buying process	• Deepen customer relationships • Customer satisfaction score • Customer retention
• Asks questions when coaching and when assessing their impact as coaches	• Asks questions when coaching and when assessing their impact as coaches	• Observes customer interactions and team selling sessions	• Describes customer successes in terms of how we discover and fulfill their needs	Sample customer responses (in addition to the previous list):	• Revenue • Product per household • Per new customer
• Encourages customer-centered results through desirable behaviors that are in alignment with team selling	• Encourages customer centered results through desirable behaviors that are in alignment with team selling	• Helps and adds value to direct reports and teams by encouraging process refinement and assisting with work arounds	• Asks value questions after every customer and team interaction	• "That was easier than I thought." • "I want to introduce you to my friends."	• Employee retention and engagement
• Reinforces employees when they share challenges and tell the truth	• Reinforces employees when they share challenges and tell the truth	• Provides feedback and recognition that reinforces desired behaviors	• Engages in team selling sessions because they want to not because they have to	• "I want to sit down and talk about my complete financial picture." • "I'd like to bring my other advisors to our meeting."	
• Holds people accountable by acknowledging and encouraging continuous incremental improvement in performance	• Holds people accountable by acknowledging and encouraging continuous, incremental improvement in performance	• Not yet fully fluent in these desired behaviors	• Not yet fully fluent in these desired behaviors	• "Tell me how to get out of a relationship with another financial institution."	
• Not yet fully fluent in these desired behaviors	• Not yet fully fluent in these desired behaviors			• "I see tremendous value in what you do." (It's not about price)	

177

CRITICAL BEHAVIORS AND RESULTS

12 MONTH VISION

Leader Behavior	Manager Behavior	Supervisor Behavior	Employee Behavior	Customer Responses	Results
• Coaches managers by providing quick and frequent feedback on what they liked and offers suggestions for incremental improvement	• Coaches supervisors by providing quick and frequent feedback on what they liked and offer suggestions for incremental improvement	• Asks questions on customer impact and the value of their coaching	• Takes full responsibility for bringing value to customers through working collaboratively with others	• Perceives us as a team of their trusted advisors	• Deepen customer relationships
• Asks questions when coaching and when assessing their impact as coaches	• Asks questions when coaching and when assessing their impact as coaches	• Observes customer interactions and team sessions	• Clearly describes customer successes in terms of how we discover and fulfill their needs	• Feels good about all parts of our organization and about the full capabilities of the organization	• Customer satisfaction score
• Encourages customer-centered results through desirable behaviors that are in alignment with the organizational strategy	• Encourages customer-centered results through desirable behaviors that are in alignment with the organizational strategy	• Helps and adds value to direct reports and teams by encouraging process refinement and assisting with work-arounds	• Asks value questions after every customer and team interaction	• Refers other opportunities to us without being asked	• Customer retention
• Reinforces employees when they share challenges and tell the truth	• Reinforces employees when they share challenges and tell the truth	• Provides feedback and recognition that reinforces desired behaviors	• Fully engages in team sessions because they want to not because they have to	• Proactively describes their longer term plans	• Revenue
• Holds people accountable by acknowledging and encouraging continuous, incremental improvement in performance	• Holds people accountable by acknowledging and encouraging continuous, incremental improvement in performance			• Openly shares risks, problems and concerns	• Product per household
					• Per new customer
					• Employee retention and engagement
					• Market share

Designing Changes

Using this tool includes clarifying what you desire for the changes not just in results and outcomes, but also in what people across all levels will be saying and doing now and in the future. This establishes results as a line of sight but also identifies behaviors that everyone will aspire to in the not-so-distant future. Start with the vision—will it be six months from now, a year from now, or two years from now? Included here are a sample of a 12-month vision and 30-, 60-, and 90-day windows. Design the end-state that includes results, customer responses and behaviors across the organization. Develop the first 30-day plan based on high-probability changes that you can make happen. What could results realistically look like in the first 30 days? What are customers likely to say or do in the first 30 days? What should employees say and do in the next 30 days to get the desired customer responses? What should employees get really good at now so that they get more of the desired customer responses? What should supervisors do to help employees in the next 30 days? And so on. This provides an initial plan and helps link your activities today to some line of sight in the distant future. It also identifies something to be impatient about—changes in behaviors and results within the first 30 days. Waiting is not allowed. Talk about grand visions is cheap. Do things today instead to create outcomes this month.

Using the Tool During a Change Effort

After you have designed the change, you can use the 30-60-90-day plan for each time period and to revise your expectations. This guide can help you track your progress and revise your plan over time. I worked with a leader who spoke eloquently about the vision of change using some of the language in the 12-month vision. He also spoke in the beginning about his near-term focus and was also able to see the connection from the 30-day plan to the 12-month vision. He kicked off this work in a genuine way but also in a concise and precise way that included not only the grand strategy but the tactics.

After filling out the guide, he was able to say what he was going to do to help move change along, not in some distant future but over each of the next four weeks. He also shared that he would be patient about many of the business results but that he would be impatient about the attempts at change. At one point, as he was reviewing the plan about 60 days into the process, he said that he thought we were being too aggressive about business results. He joked that he couldn't believe that he—a numbers guy—was slowing it down. He was right of course. The team was being too ambitious in the beginning. He made adjustments. If he did not, then he would get some reporting that looked good on paper but would not reflect what was really happening. The guide was used by this highly effective leader and his team of direct reports. They talked about it at least every other week as they reflected on their behaviors and the progress they were making.

Cautions and Additional Tip

The behavioral vision with its 30 days through 12-month view can be overwhelming, but it is less overwhelming when you work with it and understand it better. In its simplest form, it is a now-and-later chart that includes results and behaviors. The important part is to connect behaviors today to near-term and long-term results. This tool also helps ensure that behaviors are part of the future vision. It includes behaviors that become more consistent and effective over time. The results shift from what can be observed now to some of the long-term results that take quarters and years to measure.

This tool provides a way to summarize the rapid change process. Embedded within it are many of the behaviors and techniques you have been wrestling with throughout the course of this book. Now what? Take some action today. What will you personally do now to take some action moving forward?

CHAPTER 12

NOW WHAT?

Rapid change is woven right into the fabric of the organization and ensures accountability across all levels of the organization so that the change process works, helps and is sustainable. Do not be content waiting months and years to address the changes you want. Take pride in figuring out how to bring about observable, deliberate change on a daily and weekly basis.

The tactics of rapid change emerged in response to a challenging work environment. This kind of work environment, unfortunately, is not unique. Many individuals and organizations are now burdened with the need to do more with less. Business leaders have less patience and an increasing frustration with taking too long to address an issue, solve a problem or do something that has impact. They also face changes from their customers and the marketplace that are likely to have a lasting impact on their industry. This method provides a way to manage through the challenges in a proactive, progressive and repeatable way.

There is a need to do more than just manage the exceptions and problems in the workplace. Dealing with problems may be the appropriate strategy for some situations, but that is a minimally effective management strategy and will not help organizations and leaders be competitive. The economic issues today require all employees to operate at a high level of optimal performance, where all performers are providing discretionary effort. This type of work environment also requires managers and leaders who are able to guide employees and help them not only be successful with their work and customers today but to get better on a daily and weekly basis.

Why did you read this book? I hope you found the answers to the original reasons. Managers and leaders do many things in a day, week or month. The process of rapid change helps leaders attend to the few things that actually bring about desired outcomes. It assists them in how they use words to shape and guide—speaking concisely, precisely and specifically about the essential behaviors that drive implementation and execution. It directs leaders to the one to two things in the short term that make a sustainable, long-term impact. This requires a daily and weekly focus that adds up to good months, which add up to good quarters and trimesters, and then good years and successful careers. Rapid change requires focus on the here and now of this day and this week, but sustainable change requires a clear focus on a good path forward. The rapid change process also helps you discover what is hiding in plain sight—the *behaviors* that influence and sustain meaningful change.

ACKNOWLEDGMENTS

This book would not be in its present form if not for the assistance of others. I'd like to thank Gail Snyder once again for her guidance and assistance as she edited previous versions of this manuscript. James Omedo and Lisa Smith turned the words and concepts into useful graphics and cover art. Laura Lee Glass provided guidance along the way. Julie Terling assisted with marketing. Several individuals provided comments on previous versions of this book. They are Linda Mahan, Dan Gallagher, Rich Gold, Michelle Zupancic, Aubrey Daniels, Tom Spencer, Bart Sevin, Mark Repkin, Mike Bogenschutz, Cindy Ashworth and Tracy Morris. Three readers provided very detailed feedback and line editing suggestions. I owe a special thanks to them—Rob Mahan, Bill Laipple and Darnell Lattal. I'd also like to thank my clients who taught me. The following clients are included as good examples in the text. They include Pat Milantoni, James Henry, Dan Haer, Jim Burke, Mike Bogenschutz and Linda Mahan. I got the better part of the deal. Thank you for the collaboration and the partnership.

ABOUT THE AUTHOR

JOE LAIPPLE

Joseph S. Laipple, Ph.D., is a recognized thought leader in the area of coaching and leadership, team development, and change management and acceleration. He is an expert consultant who works with clients to lead and perform in strategically compelling ways that build sustainable change and accountability across all levels of the organization.

Joe has worked in a variety of industries, including pharmaceutical and biotech, banking, telecommunications, call centers and manufacturing. He has successfully worked with diverse employee populations and organizational issues, including coaching leaders on how to stay focused on strategically important results during significant transition points such as mergers and change initiatives.

Joe is the author of *Precision Selling: A Guide for Coaching Sales Professionals.* He has authored articles in applied problem solving, team building and assessments.

Joe earned his Ph.D. in psychology from West Virginia University and currently resides in Pittsburgh, PA.

ABOUT ADI

Regardless of your industry or expertise, one thing remains constant—people power your business. At Aubrey Daniels International (ADI), we work closely with the world's leading organizations to accelerate their business performance by accelerating and sustaining the performance of the men and women whose efforts drive their success. We partner with our clients in a direct, practical and sustainable way to get results faster and to increase organizational agility in today's unforgiving environment.

Founded in 1978, and headquartered in Atlanta, GA, we work with such diverse clients as Aflac, Duke Energy, Lafarge, Malt-O-Meal, M&T Bank, Medco, NASA, Genentech, Sears, FithThird Bank, Comcast and Tecnatom to systematically shape discretionary effort—where people consistently choose to do more than the minimum required. Our work with clients turns their strategy into action. We accomplish this not by adding new initiatives to their list, but by helping them make choices that are grounded in an ethical approach to people and business, by increasing effective and timely decision-making and by establishing a culture of respect for each person's contribution, regardless of rank.

Whether at an individual, departmental or organizational level, ADI provides tools and methodologies to help move people toward positive, results-driven accomplishments.

ADI's products and services help anyone improve their business:

Assessments: scalable, scientific analyses of systems, processes, structures, and practices, and their impact on individual and organizational performance

Coaching for Rapid Change®: a process for focusing managers and leaders to get change to occur now

Surveys: a complete suite of proprietary surveys to collectactionable feedback on individual and team performance, culture, safety, and other key drivers of business outcomes

Certification: ADI-endorsed mastery of client skills in the training, coaching, and implementation of our key products, processes, and/or technology

Seminars: a variety of engaging programs of practical tools and strategies for shaping individual and organizational success

Scorecards & Incentive Pay: an objective and results-focused alternative to traditional incentive pay systems

Safety Solutions: a robust suite of services to build and sustain a culture of safe habits

Expert Consulting: custom, hands-on direction and support from seasoned behavioral science professionals in the design and execution of business-critical strategies and tactics

Speakers: accredited and celebrated thought leaders

who can deliver the messages your organization needs on topics such as sustaining your gains, accelerating performance, and bringing out the best in others

aubreydaniels.com
aubreydanielsblog.com
facebook.com/Aubrey.Daniels.International
twitter.com/aubreydaniels
youtube.com/aubreydaniels